RUDI: THE FINAL MOMENTS

and

THE DANCING MAN

Two Short Novels
by Stuart Perrin

PERRIN PRESS
New York, NY

PERRIN PRESS
2109 Broadway, #3-65
New York NY 10023

Cover & book design by Robert Sink
webworksnyc.com

Cover photo used by permission
Photo by Al Rubin, courtesy of Dean Gitter

Additional photos from the DVD *Rudi: The Teachings of Swami Rudrananda* used by permission
rudimovie.org

Crash site photo used by permission
courtesy of Claudio Musajo
claudiomusajo.com

ISBN: 978-1463765309

The First Edition was originally published in 1993 by Carvalhosa Graphics under the title *The Dancing Man & A Deeper Sense of Surrender...*

To Rudi

Acknowledgments

I would like to thank Robert Sink for his tireless work in designing and layout of this Second Edition, and for pushing me to re–edit and complete both *Rudi: The Final Moments* and *The Dancing Man*; I would also like to thank both Alice Stipak and Anne Kohlstaedt for the brilliant copy–editing job they did on both stories. I would like to thank Kristina Jones for her support, and my daughter, Ania, who brightens my life every day.

I would also like to acknowledge and thank all those who worked on the First Edition: Fernando Carvalhosa, who did the original design and layout; Martine Bellen, who was the original editor of *A Deeper Sense of Surrender...*; and Keitha Capouya, who was the first editor of *The Dancing Man*.

Other Books by Stuart Perrin:

Moving On: Finding Happiness in a Changed World

A Deeper Surrender: Notes on a Spiritual Life

Leah: A Story of Meditation and Healing

The Mystical Ferryboat

Author's Preface To The First Edition

The following two novellas are linked together by a common thread. They are both rite–of–passage stories in which the deaths of a parent and of a teacher force the young protagonists to reexamine their inner lives. *The Dancing Man* explores the relationship of Joshua and his paternal father. *Rudi: The Final Moments*, originally published in the First Edition as *A Deeper Sense of Surrender...*, explores the dynamics between myself and Rudi, my spiritual father, who died in an airplane crash in 1973.

For many years, I ran an antique store in Manhattan. People would come in, see Rudi's picture on my desk, and tell me stories about how he died. I rarely said anything, but in my silence I'd remember the plane crash and the last moments of my teacher's life. I kept these memories in my heart. I didn't want to embarrass others by telling how I was in the plane with Rudi, that I heard his last words, that I'm alive because he passed his soul force into my body at the moment of impact. I am a living miracle, and I'm grateful to my spiritual father for the life he gave me.

My paternal father died when I was sixteen. His clear, radiant eyes, his depth of surrender, of spirit, love and forgiveness, and his total resignation to God's will during his last hours, made me question why he lived his whole healthy life relatively unhappy. Before passing on, he transformed himself into my spiritual teacher, though I didn't recognize it until much later. His death sparked my search for Rudi. Even at sixteen, I knew I needed to find someone who could teach me how to transform my chaotic inner world into one filled with peace and harmony. I didn't want to wait for my own death rattle to find my connection to God. Nine years later, in a small Manhattan antique shop, I met my spiritual father.

Rudi: The Final Moments and *The Dancing Man* are two chapters from the story of my life. I joyfully share them with the reader of this book and hope I shed a small light on how the spiritual process unfolds in a human being. Both stories speak to the perplexed human soul, peering out from a dark inner chamber at *Siva* dancing on the streets of New York City.

Stuart Perrin
October 5, 1993

Author's Preface To The Second Edition

Eighteen years have passed since I first published the book now called *Rudi: The Final Moments.* Not only have I changed, but my writing style has changed, my teachings have changed, and it seems to me as if the very complex understanding I once had of the world has simplified itself, and what was far–fetched and beyond reach has found expression in my day–to–day life. At the center of it all is Rudi. I remember being grateful to him for allowing me to be present at the moment of his passing; I remember thinking that up to this point it's been easy. The future will show me whether or not I truly learned what he tried to teach me. He told me many times that the guru lives in the disciple's heart. It's perhaps why I never felt great loss. From the very moment he took his Samadhi, I found him sitting in full lotus position at the center of my heart. It was like he had always been there — a remarkable being guiding me through the complicated evolution of my life.

Very few people understand the dynamic that takes place between a spiritual teacher and a disciple. This is perhaps, the most sacred marriage on earth — a mystical union that's essential for both their enlightenments. It's also a means the universe uses to pass down spiritual teachings from generation to generation. It should never be taken for granted.

Most important, spiritual teachers live low-keyed lives. They spend their time surrendering ego. I remember Rudi telling me that he had never forgotten the great Hindu saint Swami Nityananda sleeping on a potato sack. He told me that the simplicity of Swami Nityananda's life inspired him to work hard on himself to get closer to God. "Someday," Rudi said to me," I'll become simple enough to live with nothing."

The story of his death is so dramatic that just telling it makes good literature. The clear day, the densest fog I'd ever seen, the roar of the airplane motor, Rudi's dictation, my mind moving from the present to the past and back again, the entire journey had an allegorical ring to it; and Rudi, who had told me many times that he would live to eighty-four, said his last words, "...a deeper sense of surrender," and was taken by the hand of God. He was forty-five years old.

From the moment that I wrote this book, I thought it had something important to teach people on the spiritual path. With this in mind, I decided to republish it under the title of *Rudi: The Final Moments*. With gratitude I re-offer this book to a reading public and hope some of its words inspire readers to go into themselves and excavate the vast treasure house of love and wisdom that's hidden deep inside every human being.

Stuart Perrin
October 5, 2011

RUDI: THE FINAL MOMENTS

Introduction

In many ways, *Rudi: The Final Moments* conceived itself. After writing *Leah, The Mystical Ferryboat*, and *The Dancing Man*, I found myself sitting at my desk wading through sketches and notes that were seeds of a story trying to sprout. And as I labored year after year over draft after draft, the difficulty of writing *Rudi: The Final Moments* became apparent to me: I was attempting to communicate and share, with an unknown reader, the single most dramatic experience of my life — a story I never wanted to write in the first place, an experience I thought almost impossible to relive.

The incident itself occurred on February 21, 1973. On the surface it was simple enough: a small plane took off from Teeterboro airport in New Jersey on its way to Glens Falls, a small town near Albany. It was lost in fog and crashed into a mountain. One person died and three survived. But superficial narrative does little to convey the depth of the experience. The person who died was Rudi, my spiritual teacher, my guru, the person I loved more than anyone in the world. I cannot imagine how I would have responded to this news if I hadn't been in the plane when it hit the mountain and seen Rudi's body surrounded by wreckage, rocks and barren trees. I never asked myself why it happened. There were simply no answers. I surprised myself by showing little or no outward emotion, never getting angry or upset. But my inner life raged like a forest fire, and I struggled to find my connection with God. I tried to adjust to life without Rudi. I forgave God and death for taking from me the person who had saved my life. I never shared my innermost thoughts and feelings. I knew that I'd have to work hard on myself to let go of Rudi; I knew that loving him meant building my own connection with Higher Creative Energy in the Universe. I needed to keep Rudi in my heart, to continue his work and climb my personal mountain to spiritual enlightenment.

I remember him saying, "The best way to serve your guru is to build your inner life, to get your own connection with God."

Rudi's meditation practice and unconditional love had helped me through the most difficult period of my life. Now that he was gone, I wanted him to dance with angels, to be a speck of light in the cosmos, to nestle himself in the bosom of God. I believed that my tears, lamentations and sorrow would only bring him back to earth — they would negate his lifetime of work and surrender.

Twenty years had passed since the plane crash. I had spent seven of those years living in Texas where I ran a meditation center. Then I returned to New York City. I would visit the crash site — to me a holy place where my spiritual teacher took his *samadhi* — once a year with many students, most of whom had never met Rudi. We'd meditate there, and during those meditations, I realized that birth and death were part of a cosmic dance. One didn't negate the other. I also realized that Rudi lived inside me. To be with him, I simply had to open my heart, love him, be loved by him, and renew my spiritual quest every day.

Writing *Rudi: The Final Moments* had its problems. A one–hour plane ride became my vehicle to explore the six–year relationship I had with Rudi: the coming of age of a young spiritual seeker; the dynamics between him and a guru who had infinite patience, infinite love, and wisdom that transcended ordinary understanding.

A stream–of–consciousness flow throughout the story connects the present to the past and back again. It contains elements of allegory as well as realism. Some people might object to this. They might wonder if I truly thought all these things while sitting in the front seat of the airplane. They might question me as to whether I'm writing fiction or fact. Yet I have found that the line between fiction and fact dissolves when the inner life of a human being is explored. In writing this story, I tried to gain insight into my relationship with Rudi — that was my objective; but like any other work of art, the story's real meaning lies in whatever the reader brings to it. The best I can do is share a microcosmic view of a spiritual quest, and that I offer to you...

February 1993

Rudi: The Final Moments

February 21, 1973, 5:40 PM. Rudi, Beau, Mimi, and I take off from Teeterboro Airport, New Jersey in a Cessna prop plane flying north to Glens Falls, New York, a small town near Albany. We fly into a clear winter's sky of muted oranges, reds and yellows, more spring-like than winter, past a sun descending over tracts of houses and cars driven through suburban neighborhoods, over roads and highways connecting village to town, over the snakelike Hudson winding its way north. The cars, trees, and houses shrink to dots among patches of yellow brown. We bounce from wind gust to wind gust, leveling off thousands of feet above the sprawling earth.

Beau is piloting the plane. Rudi and Mimi are in the back seat, Mimi behind me, and Rudi behind Beau. Beau checks the instrument panel and talks into the radio. "It's my first non-school flight," he said to me on the way to the airport. "It'll save Rudi hours of driving, give him more time to teach."

He reminds me of a kid with a new toy. I don't know him well, but enjoy his iconoclastic irreverence — a rebel taking the highroad to nowhere as though lost in a Joseph Conrad novel and not wanting to find his way out. I know that Rudi loves him and that Beau loves the strength and sheer majesty of Rudi, who has helped him unknot the tangled rope of his life. Mimi, his girlfriend, I met in acting school seven or eight years ago. We lost touch and were reintroduced at Rudi's ashram.

I look out the side window. No snow, I think. The reservoir will dry up, the brooks and streams will dry up. There'll be a drought this summer. They'll pipe water into New York City from the Hudson, water filled with chemicals poisoning thirsty New Yorkers, transforming the city into a ghost town. Just concrete streets, brick and glass buildings — no movement, no people, nothing...

The altimeter reads eight thousand feet.

New York's water is the best in the world, I muse. They bottle it and sell it at Macy's.

The things I think about when I've nothing to do.

But the mind doesn't shut up, especially in a fragile Cessna where jolts of fear shoot through my heart and belly. Nothing can happen, I think, because Rudi's in the back seat. He's getting ready to dictate to Mimi. We'll land in about an hour or so. Anyway, he said he'd live to be eighty–four. That's thirty–nine more years. He said that he has teachings to give, work to do, that dying is the easy way out. I take a deep breath, turn to Rudi, and back to the instrument panel: 125MPH/8000 feet. It's all right to unhook my seat belt. I'll be more comfortable. What can happen if Rudi's here? "There are more small plane crashes than any other type," a voice says inside me. I breathe into my navel *chakra*, center myself, shake off the voice, take Rudi's hand and listen to him dictate:

"These last two weeks I knew I was going through a transition, but could not determine which way it would carry me."

The plane climbs past 8500 feet. I wonder how high the Rocky Mountains are? The Catskills? The Empire State Building? Beau fiddles with the instrument panel. Rudi squeezes my hand. How clear the sky is, I think. How vast and infinite are its shades of blue. There are only small patches of clouds on the western horizon, clouds covering the setting sun, creating fantastic images and shapes. I turn to Rudi.

"I'm glad you're here," he says.

"Me too," I answer.

"We've been together for a long time."

"Six years," I say with a smile on my face.

Six years ago, I walked into his antique store and knew that my search for a spiritual teacher had come to an end. Six years ago, a homeless child wandered into his father's heart, finding shelter, love, room to breathe, spiritual guidance and God; a place to work out my fear, anger, and unhappiness, to rid myself of dark, tortured thoughts, and to learn the slow process of coming of age. The struggle of life rang in my ear like a bell ringing in an ancient temple, a bell sounding: I am with God...the city, sea and earth are with God...the sun and sky are with God — all a solo voice shouting from the eye of a hurricane, etching daily events into the mind of the universe. For the first time I recognized that "one plus one" equals two or three depending on my frame of reference. Before meeting Rudi, my drug–infested brain — a brain lost in self–induced, cloud-like fantasies, had played out all the petty dramas.

"The outer world is a mirror image of the inner," Rudi said. "If we open within ourselves, if we get past our tensions, if we surrender our ideas of right and wrong, and learn to recognize that all of life reflects our inner condition..."

The outer world once scared the shit out of me, I muse, a big, bad–

assed world dressed in Day-Glo clothing and dancing a mambo in the sky. As a child, I hid from it. I crawled under beds, behind stairwells and, once, I climbed into a chest of drawers. I thought the outer world had nothing to teach me. I knew more than it did. But six years ago, the outer world forced me to crawl to Rudi. "You've got to enjoy it," Rudi always said. "Take its skirt off. Jump in. If you don't experience the world, there'll be nothing to surrender."

I remember when Wendy Steinberg lifted her dress above her head and sang, "Come out! Come out, wherever you are!" I was five years old at the time with a pillow under my head and a blanket over my face. She kept singing, "Come out!" and I kept burying my face in the blanket.

I study the Hudson's northern extension and count car headlights. The sun darts behind clouds. It creates shadows over tracts of land, and lights reflect off the western sky, painting the horizon the ethereal colors found in Altdorfer's Battle of Issus. I let my mind wander into the realm of fairy tale and saga. Great armies march into cities glittering with gold and silver arches, minarets, spires and temples. Knights slay dragons, and fiery, multi-armed and legged creatures embrace the earth in a wild and uncontrollable dance. They wear beaded necklaces that resemble human heads, crowns with skulls, flayed leopard-skin shawls, and have blue bodies, red faces, legs like tigers and widespread wings. Clouds become whatever I want them to be: a woman's naked body curved across the horizon; a portrait of my mother or father; an animal hunting prey; a bird stretching its wings thirty miles across the sky. I remember taking a path into remote corners of my own mind, where shifting cloud forms disappeared into vast and endless nothingness...

"To learn to surrender is to learn to transform ego into nothingness," Rudi said to me one day while he sat in half-lotus position at his antique store desk. Above him, beside him and beneath him were Oriental works of art. He sat perfectly at ease, like the incarnation of the Buddha himself — a rosy-cheeked Buddha born in East New York and raised in Brownsville — a bagels-and-lox Buddha that transformed the city into his own unique vision of the Bodhi Tree.

He tied a clasp to a necklace he had just strung and asked me to get him a cup of coffee.

"I'm tired," he said when I returned. "Sometimes I feel like a bullock going round and round a well, a bullock schlepping myself and my students with me. I've been working on this side of exhaustion for as long as I can remember." He smiled and went on. "But we're here to work ourselves free of karma. You know the difference between most people and me?" he asked. "I'm willing to do what's necessary to get to God. I know my priorities. Nothing keeps me from doing my inner work. Nothing is more important than serving God."

On the way out of his store, I repeated to myself: "I'm a child. I know so little about life. There are thousands of subtle vibrations keeping me off balance, making my world an almost unbearable place to live. I can't separate the inner from the outer, reality from illusion."

Rudi's fingers tighten around my hand and draw me out of my reverie. It's getting darker. Wisps of cloud create configurations around the plane. It's like flying through interwoven threads on a tapestry — translucent threads made of light, threads without density and without barriers. I can barely see the Hudson. I can't tell if we're over New Jersey or New York. It all looks the same to me: patches of lawn, pastures and clumps of trees, people embracing generic lifestyles, hiding in safe and remote precincts. I've always wanted to live in fabulous cities and take extended voyages. I've paid homage to artists and writers such as Bosch, Altdorfer, Blake, Baudelaire, and Rimbaud — men not afraid to traverse the dark regions of the human soul where the child in us plays at the edge of the world, where light and color are ethereal projections emanating from hidden wellsprings, where overactive imaginations destroy all boundaries...

"I've got lots of hours in the air," Beau says to me, but I don't answer. I can feel Rudi's hand in mine while I continue looking for vague outlines of the Hudson's extension. There's got to be a place where the water's still pure, I muse, a place where fish live and wildlife drink from the riverbank.

"Fear is healthy if we don't let it get out of control," Rudi said one day while we sat together in his store. "Fear reminds us that we're human. What's the worst that can happen to us? We die? Then there's no more pain, suffering or sorrow. Our fear goes away. We no longer struggle to find answers. We go on vacation. But why worry while there's still plenty of karma to work out? If you let fear take over your mind, it'll cripple you. The best thing is to starve it to death, to let it dry up inside you."

Someday I'll feel at home on the earth, I think, someday I'll experience a moment of quiet.

"I have been sitting all day," Rudi continues to dictate to Mimi, "letting negative psychic tension flow through my fingers which it has been doing with increasing intensity."

He sat day after day, year after year, in a Greenwich Village Oriental art emporium, selling old and new artifacts from the East.

There are many shops in New York City, but none like Rudi's, where wisdom, love, and spiritual teachings are dispensed between sales, where the material and spiritual harmoniously wrap their arms around each other. The Buddha lives in Rudi's store; *Siva* dances there; all the gods and demigods in the Hindu and Buddhist pantheon celebrate the wonders of creation. It's a temple if I'd ever been in a temple, where New York City street wisdom marries Oriental mysticism and gives birth every day to a prodigal son named Rudi.

"God sends me my students," Rudi once said. "I have no say in this. It doesn't matter what their physical or psychological condition is. What matters is that they want to grow, that they want to have a spiritual life. If that need is real, then they qualify for my classes. I remember my own emotional and mental condition when I was younger. My teachers accepted me. If they didn't, I'd be dead today."

Before I met Rudi, I listened to a screaming voice in my head that had all and none of the answers at the same time. In the beginning, a mentally-crippled and unhappy disciple said yes to his teacher, a disciple who had no choice but to listen. I had been through ten self-indulgent years and had arrived at a place in myself where my drug-induced repertoire drove me to just this side of insanity. Then Rudi picked me off the streets.

"What happened that day?" I once asked him.

"I saw my son lost in the universe and pulled him through the door."

But sons are not what parents think they are; sons also struggle to find their own identity...

"It's a matter of energy," Rudi said to a small group of his students. He sat next to a five-foot-high Japanese bronze seated Buddha. "It's a matter of getting the spiritual food you need, of getting strong enough inside yourself to love and be loved. It's a matter of staying with spiritual work long enough to get the teachings. Endurance teaches patience. Patience teaches that you've got to listen to someone besides yourself."

What choice do I have? I thought, laughing to myself. The sea keeps switching directions. Currents of fear move in and out of my heart, and strangle my need to love and change. I have to listen to him. It's the only way to overcome myself. But easier said than done. Every time I listen to him, a voice in me shouts: "Nothing changes! The world's diseased! Big egos devour little egos. People die bitter deaths because they're incapable of loving."

A customer walks into Rudi's store.

"Can I help you?" Rudi asks him.

"Just looking," he answers.

For what? I think. People search and look and find nothing but empty spaces. I walked into this gallery and found Rudi, and he became my connection to God. How blind most people are! How they refuse to see what's directly in front of their noses!

Sometimes I think Rudi's job is finding life where most people are afraid to look. I always wonder how he does it. It's like raising Lazarus from the dead, like scraping barnacles from the hull of a rusty ship...

He told me to internalize my vision, to experience an evolving vortex of energy, to transform all my tension into a positive force.

"Tension is just human garbage," he said, "and garbage makes the best compost. If you bring your tension to the third *chakra* and transform it into energy, the thing that's killing you will give you life. It's a way of using all your inner crap to break out of a self-imposed prison and make room for God. Like an alchemist, we have to transform everything into gold."

My first six months with Rudi were a time of loving innocence. They were like idyllic days in a brand new love affair. The Guru–Disciple relationship dilly-dallied in my heart. I'd found a teacher, father, lover and friend. He took me in, had patience with me, and forgave my incompetence. I thought it would all last forever. But my mind continued to look at reflections in a mirror of its own demons. It had trouble seeing past them and forever wandered into cul–de–sacs. My mind peeked over concrete walls at open spaces filled with its own projections.

"How long does it take to become enlightened?" I asked Rudi a few months after I began to study with him.

"How long did it take to get into your condition?" he answered.

"Twenty–six years," I smiled.

"Do you think you're going to get out of it in a couple of months?" he replied. "The problem with people is that they're lazy. They want instant rewards for little or no effort. They covet the two–hour day. They treat time cheaply, and life cheaply, and take for granted the brief period we have between birth and death. They don't realize that we take out of life exactly what we invest in it. Spiritual work touches on the impossible. It has a logic all its own that transforms preconceived, opinionated, planned and orderly lifestyles into an animated cartoon in which nothing makes sense. At the show's end, most people do a clumsy two–step. As they tumble off the stage, they shrug their shoulders and sing in off–key voices: 'that's all folks'. Trying to make sense of life is like trying to pour the Atlantic Ocean into a coffee cup. How does one referee a wrestling match between the dead and dying parts of oneself and a life–seeking spirit that refuses to accept boring, mundane, and mediocre answers to problems? Most people clutch the former. They're strangled by insecurity and fear. They take their lives for granted."

The days merged with each other. They were timeless days that slipped past with a quickness I'd never before known. Yet Rudi seemed to have always been in my life, and his teachings were medicine for my inner turmoil. I'd listen to him speak of his own struggles, of his teacher in India, of his mother, of love affairs, and his store. As long as he could remember, he'd taken on himself high–pressure situations as a way of combating his own inert nature. His college curriculum consisted of mathematics and science courses. They were his least–favorite studies. He had no aptitude for them. But they forced him to organize his thoughts, to develop good study habits, and to work against himself.

He studied textile engineering at North Carolina State University because he knew it would be difficult to learn. He never wanted to be a textile engineer. He'd been given a scholarship, and thought that mathematics and science were just the right formula for the lazy, undisciplined person he claimed himself to be.

Six months after college, on a walk through Greenwich Village, he stopped in front of a vacant store on Seventh Avenue South. A voice in him cried out: "Rent it! Open a shop!" Years of struggle had taught him to trust his instincts. So the next day he signed a lease and opened a business selling whatever he could find to sell. Every Wednesday, he'd rent a van and scour the New York City streets for old furniture and fixtures, often one block ahead of the Sanitation Department. At night he'd wash dishes at the Village Vanguard to earn money to pay his store rent and feed himself.

His father had skipped out on his mother when Rudi was very young. He left her in abject poverty with three kids to bring up. They never saw him again. His mother put food on the table and gave them a place to sleep. She did it against impossible odds. Rudi learned early on that no matter what she did to him, she was still his mother, and, even today, he never forgot that he was responsible for loving her. That's what she needed from him.

He began working at age thirteen and had continued working ever since. But for him the past was dead. He fought his way out of it. The idea of going back was so frightening that it made him work harder at building his life today. There was only the present and the future, and the future was simply the present unfolding itself.

The difference between us is astonishing, I think. We're two aliens sharing common ground. I had spent most of my life avoiding work and responsibility, believing them to be society's wish to imprison me in an economic conundrum. I used to think that society eats, digests, and spits out humanity. It molds people into assembly line clones of one another. So I went from job to job, relationship to relationship, and country to country. I invested my time and energy in literature, art, and music, and imagined them to be a direct route to God. Money was a symbol that played on people's insatiable need for success and power. It provided neither love nor joy nor happiness. It ripped the lifeblood and creative force out of people's guts. I didn't want to be weighed down by finances. I cared little about power and success. I had once read in the New Testament, "Give unto Caesar what is Caesar's, give unto God what is God's" — and decided that Caesar loomed too large in the minds and hearts of most people. Nothing more had to be given to him. If I paid my rent, ate and lived simply, I could give my soul to art and literature. I smoked grass, took hallucinogens, and embraced a transcendental world in which God and Caesar couldn't coexist. I plumbed the depths of my inner being, had visions and insights, saw God in His many *Tantric* manifestations, and meditated on cosmic light and color. Only my mind refused to shut up. It drove me to distraction; it filled me with perverse and elevated dialogues — a rapid succession of montage–like images, one more bizarre than the other. My head ached, my chest hurt, and at no time did I feel balance, harmony, and love; my one–bedroom railroad flat felt more like St. Anthony's cave than a home.

Then I met Rudi. I was three weeks out of a Spanish prison and four days from most likely entering an asylum when Rudi pulled me off the streets. It seemed to me that my heart opened for the first time. I remember sitting on a hardwood bench in a jail cell with a copy of the *Bhagavad Gita* in my hand. I stared at an exposed toilet opposite me that looked like a piece of conceptual art and thought that it doesn't get worse than this. I had taken myself to the bottom. I prayed a lot, asked for help, and kissed the ground when they finally let me out. Three weeks later, the heart of the universe opened to me. I found

Rudi dancing at its center — a smile on his face and words of wisdom coming out of his mouth.

"No more dope," he said to me the second day after I met him. Thank God, I thought as we walked east on Tenth Street to his meditation center between Third and Fourth Avenues.

Before I knew it, the idyllic Rudi days ended as suddenly as they began and I entered a new phase of the Guru–Disciple relationship — a stage likened to riding a river raft over strong currents. The water became treacherous and difficult to navigate. Deep pockets of anger surfaced, along with jealousy, fear, and frustration — emotions buried deep inside me unearthed themselves and stared me in the face, emotions I'd forgotten about, that I'd desensitized myself to, that were like stagnant pools of water activated by violent winds. Rudi pushed me into the water. He forced me to dredge up ancient hurts. He transformed a sad but calm person into a muddy swamp of buried pain. My anger and jealousy almost drove me crazy. I lived for six months in a no man's land populated by my own demon–filled self. I had never before realized how screwed up I was. I had never faced my fear head on. Ten times daily I asked myself why I needed a guru, why I couldn't just live in a monastery or cave and forget the crazy "me" I kept seeing in the mirror. I cried, I vomited, I got sick, paralyzed, and suffered acute headaches. I could barely function. My dreams populated themselves with snakelike creatures that wrapped themselves around my heart, and with flocks of gorgon–headed birds eating my liver. I saw in them great rivers of blood that flowed from my midsection, and I'd often see my flayed body hanging from a clothesline to dry. My inner world seethed with open wounds that were sore and festering — a nerve ending touched by every stimulus, I was afraid of living, of hiding in dark shadows, of running from the truth. I fought an inner battle with Rudi. He talked to me about resistance, about change, about struggling with death.

"All spiritual work is based on dying and being reborn," he said. "It's a constant struggle, a battle to transcend oneself. If you endure, you'll get your enlightenment."

There was no way that I could return to my former life. I could only go on. But I felt like a water buffalo pulling a cart on a hot and dusty Indian dirt road. All the baggage of a lifetime weighed heavily on my shoulders. I kept saying to myself that I was in Rudi's ashram to have a spiritual life. I needed to be healed; I needed to be guided through my fragile world.

"It's foolish to run away," Rudi once said. "Your environment might change, your activities might change, but no matter where you run to, when you look in the mirror, you'll still see yourself."

But the changes compounded themselves minute by minute until my mind, body and spirit collided, and I lived at the center of a seemingly–endless void. I'd think that there was too much to surrender. My body was getting old, my mind's chitchat never stopped; the earth kept spinning, the stars, moon and sun — all permanent fixtures in the heavens — all changing moment by moment. Nothing was real and there was nothing to hang on to and nowhere to go. My fragmented thoughts crippled me, and it became apparent that spiritual work and insanity made handsome bedfellows. I could barely distinguish between the two.

"We've got to learn that all creative energy exists in the unknown," Rudi once said. "Mostly our knowledge is limited to our understanding and our minds are like grains of sand on a beach…"

Thousands of windblown grains bouncing off each other, changing positions and ground into particles of dust by the ceaseless and repetitious beating of the surf. The ocean eats continents, streams devour mountains, mountains erupt — time alone understands beginnings and endings. The rest of life is a shifting and changing zealous force that never seems to rest.

"Human beings are creatures of habit," Rudi said to me one afternoon in his store. "They resist change and hold on to the familiar, even if it's going to kill them. They're afraid to let go, because letting go means dealing with the new and unexplored. We even hold on to our neurosis. If we're crazy, we can always excuse ourselves, we have a reason not to function. I mean change also affects us on basic levels. How many times have you found yourself trying to change toothpastes or shaving creams; how many times have you found yourself standing for at least a half hour in front of a shelf of dental products in a pharmacy, trying to make a decision? It's laughable. But life's familiar imprint represents a safety zone for us — a kind of leash we tie around our necks."

I've been boxing fifteen rounds a day for thirty years of my life against heavyweight opponents in a ring located somewhere in the far precincts of my mind, I think while looking out the front window of the plane. It's a no contest bout. Sooner or later I'm going to get knocked out; sooner or later I'll be ground to dust. I keep saying to myself: "Let go. You can't win the battle. What can happen? Just let go."

"The real battlefield of truth is inside each and every one of us," Rudi said to me one morning while we were walking through the streets of

Manhattan. "We're caught between two poles, one pulling us towards death and malaise, the other forcing us to seek light. We're walking a tightrope of sorts that requires perfect balance and harmony. Whether or not we survive the battle depends on how hungry we are to have a spiritual life."

The love I need peeks out of Rudi's heart, I think. I've got to be with him. He's my nipple…

"True independence is the realization that we are dependent on everyone and everything," Rudi continued as we crossed Second Avenue. "A child is born, weaned, sent out to the world..."

Someday I'll walk on my own two feet. But, for now, thank God for the guru's tit. Hiding behind a great deal of pain, my childlike self seeks spiritual enlightenment — a homeless self drifting in thoughts of God and spirituality, a self alien to life — it's restless, uncomfortable and afraid to leave the darkness. Rudi peels my masks away. He makes me build bridges connecting my inner and outer lives.

"There's no separation," he once said. "Only the mind creates separation; only the mind puts things in little boxes. Your tension is energy. You've got to learn to transform it into a life–giving force."

Memories are energy. Fog is energy. A plane moving through the sky is energy.

The muted sunset disappears behind mountainous clouds in the west. Traces of fog roll over the plane. Beau takes us to ten thousand feet.

The sky's a playground for poets and artists, a place for dreamers to lose themselves in changing form and color, a beautiful place, illusive, incomprehensible, always there, a reminder that life and death are fragile, interwoven threads on a vast, invisible loom. No poet can quite grasp its beauty; no artist can truly paint its mysterious elegance, no voice can sing its true essence. The sky's intangible self reminds me of nature's perfection, and of human frailty. Sometimes, I think, it's nothing but God laughing at us from on high.

But "Nothings" are futile "What if's?" when human beings think about them. "Nothings" blur my memory and paralyze my thoughts. They make me feel like a child lost in the world. I was six once. I heard a voice say "Rudi." He came to me nineteen years later.

To be "Nothing" is a state of grace, they say; when you're "Nothing" you're filled with God. Somehow, they say many things that only make sense when I'm in a state of surrender, and, somehow, sense and nonsense are the same when we meditate on "Nothingness."

"Creative people won't let themselves be shackled by ideologies and institutions," Rudi said one day while we sat outside his Seventh Avenue South store. "They're irreverent, sacrilegious, slightly mad, and they stubbornly refuse to be sucked dry by dogma. It's virtually impossible to become God–realized when trapped in institutions that pose as houses of worship. It's why I've never gone non–profit. I'm afraid if my ashram gets institutionalized, I'll be the first to quit." He took a deep breath, smiled, and continued talking. "It's like trying to plot out a day in one's life. You wake up in the morning, get out of bed, and schedule your day's events. Within five minutes the phone rings. It's your girlfriend, mother, boss, or some long-lost friend, and suddenly the day is different. Ten minutes later the electricity blows out or the water pipes leak or the phone goes dead or a bird shits on your head, and you stand center stage to all this drama asking, 'Why me? What have I done to deserve this?' We refuse to recognize that life's real test is taking out the garbage with an open heart. We're masters at bitching and complaining, but complete fools when it comes to dealing with life's unexpected pressures.

"From birth to death, unforeseen events ruffle our well–made beds," Rudi continued to talk. It was early afternoon and many people strolled past his shop on Seventh Avenue South. "Events that are almost like mosquitoes stinging us in the dark. We can't just shrug them off. They test our patience, balance, and well-being. We entrench ourselves, and with bayonets in hand, we try to kill thousands of these mosquito–like events that follow us through life. We're driven to houses of prayer where we kneel and bow, and complain about our existence, where we fill our minds with lament–ridden monologues that make God run for cover. I'm sure that all the gods and demigods have healthy supplies of cotton to stuff in their ears. I'm sure they're tired of all the *kvetching* on the earth. If one human being offers up a little gratitude, the entire cosmos bursts into song. Trumpets sound, gongs, bells, and drums play joyful melodies, and the Divine Symphony Orchestra makes music too beautiful for words. You see, on the other side of each and every one of us is spiritual enlightenment. All we've got to do is get free of our self to be with God."

How true! How frighteningly true, I think while I continue to look out the plane window. The sun peeps out like a papier mâché disc dangling just above the horizon. I marvel how man's intrepid genius invents machines that fly thousands of feet above the earth and give us access to paradisiacal realms.

"There are no two people alike," said Rudi that afternoon on the Seventh Avenue South sidewalk. "But our commonality is that every person needs to be loved. Even hardened criminals touch life the only way they know how. They steal love from the world, killing, robbing an indifferent society that's withheld its love from them since birth. They become wards of a giant shit hole of a prison system that feeds and houses hundreds of thousands of society's spiritually undernourished children. They're reminded every day of how stupid they are and how guilty. I mean no one wants to crawl out of a hole to be bludgeoned with wisdom that makes no sense."

Certainly not a wise man whose life has been spent learning to detach his heart and mind from a looney-tune parade of non-sequiturs, I think as the plane moves from cloud to cloud. The voice of wisdom is in silence, and it circles the globe like a tortoise swimming from sea to sea. The voice of silence teaches patience and forgiveness. It teaches us to listen to other people.

As a child, Rudi's need to be with God transcended his other needs. He read palms. He discovered he had ESP, and often believed himself to be half mad and an outcast on earth. He saw orange-robed specters sitting on his bed and they taught him the ways of God.

"I'd open my hand," he once said to me in the living room of his loft on East Tenth Street, "and a lama would be perched on each finger. The Buddha would be sitting at the center of my palm. I was seven years-old at the time and thought I was going mad. Later on, these orange-robed lamas told me that to get to God I would have to work. They repeated again and again that work brings more work until we finally work our way out of the world. I received my Tibetan Buddhist education at an early age, but I was afraid to talk about it. My private world hinged on psychic and spiritual experience. Somehow, I knew my life would be special; somehow I knew that I'd been born to serve God."

The idea of a guru being born in Brooklyn strikes an absurd note in my mind, I think as I look out the plane window at gathering clouds. Holy men are not supposed to be raised on the streets of East New York and the South Bronx. But, then I think: why not? Surviving a South Bronx and East New York childhood and fighting one's way out of these rough neighborhoods is nothing short of a miracle. It's not the environment, per se, but the lower middle-class security ethic that traps people in economic, religious, and social grooves — like Sisyphus pushing a stone up a mountain.

The winter's snow didn't come this year. The earth is dark and gray, and the trees are barren. I take Rudi's hand. Jolts of spiritual energy shoot up my arm into the center of my chest. My back arches, my head swivels, and I close my eyes. He chuckles in the back seat.

"I'm a cow," he once said to me in the Second Avenue Deli. "I've got big tits and they need to be milked. But, it's hard finding someone who's thirsty. A teacher needs to give his teachings away. They're his last karmic barrier, and if he doesn't, they'll dry up and choke him. An aura of mystery surrounds spiritual work. Arcane answers are dangled before students like sugar before a horse. But the real mystery to me is why people won't work hard enough on themselves to build a direct connection to God, why people allow the *chakra* system to atrophy and become useless? The answers are always in front of our noses. We just have to see them. They are rarely in great cosmic revelations, but in cows that give milk, in big tits that need to be suckled by thirsty students. Sometimes my nipples hurt so badly I could cry. If you drink, Stuart, if you learn what I've got to teach, you'll never need another guru. I'll give you everything."

At times, I'm like a river rock trying to absorb water, I muse as I observe from the plane's window dark cloud formations forming in front of us. At other times, I'm so pregnant with spiritual energy, it's as if I'm ready to give birth.

"To digest the bulk of my teachings in one gulp," Rudi went on after ordering a couple of franks with the works at the Second Avenue Deli, "is like trying to feed a twenty–two ounce steak to a starving person. It's best to nibble at my *shakti*, to slowly strengthen your *chakra* system, and to build inner balance. As you get stronger, your spiritual digestive system requires more roughage. You can take much bigger bites out of the *shakti* and go deeper into yourself. It's funny how today I accomplish in seconds what once took me years."

After one Saturday morning meditation class, I eagerly presented to him a few of my insights, and I told him how important they were to me, and how strong my connection was to God. He looked at me with tongue in cheek and said softly to a friend of his sitting next to him, "The schmuck thinks he's having a spiritual life. How long have you been studying with me?" he asked. "About a year," I answered. He just shrugged his shoulders and smiled. "I've been doing this for thirty–six years," he said, "and still haven't a notion of what it's all about."

Sometimes I believe I'm destined to spend my entire life in the ghetto of Schmuck–dom, I thought, as I swallowed my anger and pride and took a seat near Rudi. I eat wisdom like saltpeter, dispense thoughts like poison arrows, review the same lessons over and over again, discover that whatever I think I know, whatever I think I've learned, and whatever I am, all must be discarded with my next breath. The Earl of Schmuck–dom surrounded by vassals, by a seneschal, by gravediggers and royal patrons, the Earl of Schmuck–dom perched on his river rock, hoping the water's pressure will erode his island and the tiny particles of his Duchy will dissolve to dust and float out to sea.

"It's not who and what we are," Rudi said his friend and me, "but what we're not. If a saint doesn't surrender his saintliness he'll never get to God." He peeled an apple, cut it into quarters, took out the core, and gave a piece to his friend and me. He put the last quarter on a plate and rested the plate on the lap of a life–size bronze Buddha seated next to him. He ate his piece with childlike relish. He dropped his arms to his sides, took a few deep breaths, closed his eyes, shook his hands, and processed tension off the ends of his fingertips. After a few minutes of practicing this exercise, he opened his eyes and said: "So much crap accumulates inside us. We're like garbage dumps. If we don't rid ourselves of tension, it backs up, congests us, and creates disease and anxiety. It poisons everything we do. If the plumbing in a house clogs up, it all comes out the kitchen sink. The *chakra* system's no different. We've got to work to cleanse it and keep our life–force flowing. If not, our tension will back up into our heads and drive us crazy."

Like Do–Do the clown in pigtails running naked through Times Square, I thought. Crazy I've been and crazy I am, but somehow it's got to stop. If my mind quits its never–ending prattle, my spiritual life will rise out of the mud.

"If you look up a cow's ass, you'll see shit," Rudi continued talking. "If you pull its tits, you get milk."

I'm tired of looking up a cow's ass at the dark side of myself; I'm tired of knowing everything and nothing. But being tired has never gotten me a goddamned thing. One thing I do know is that I've got to continue to suck Rudi's spiritual tit. God demands that I take a big bite of the guru's tit...God is...I don't know what the hell God is. Maybe that's a beginning.

So what do I do? I mused, as I looked out the plane window. Do I wait? Do I climb the mountain step by step? I have to learn patience. I have to slowly learn the ways of God on earth.

But sometimes I think God's ways are not fast enough. They don't prepare me to move quickly through a fast–paced world of media, communications and travel. Sometimes it's hard for me to believe that God exists in the twentieth century. But God is energy, life is energy, the twentieth century is energy. So therefore, God exists. But how do I learn to love Him? How do I see past the madness of life exploding all around me? If I can't communicate with myself, how am I going to talk to other people?

"The external world mirrors the inner life of every person," Rudi once said to me. We had just come out of a movie and were going into a Chinese restaurant for a bite to eat, "but no two people see the same reflection. It's better to be a spectator at life's circus; it's better to make friends with the reflections we see in the mirror. They're just ourselves looking back at us, and to struggle against a mirror image of one's self is a foolish if not hopeless battle." He picked up the menu in the restaurant and began to chuckle. "We're all like millions of bumper cars colliding with each other at different speeds," he said. "We see only what we want to see. The external world tells us exactly how foolish we are, but we're so caught up in our own thoughts that we never listen."

The dark, mountainous cloud forms in the west grow denser as we move through a light fog. I can still see traces of the Hudson River, of lit homes, streetlamps, and car headlights. The night begins settling in. It's the time of day when light and darkness struggle with each other, when there's still faint hope that day's end can be postponed and the inevitable encroachment of darkness will arrest itself and allow daylight a few extra moments.

Rudi's fast asleep and the propeller's whirring sound makes me feel drowsy. I close my eyes, but a restless, uncomfortable sensation grips my body. When my thoughts begin to race, I've trained myself to listen to my breathing, and the slow, steady rhythm of inhalation and exhalation almost always relaxes me. The noisy chatter in my mind disappears and I'm left with only silence.

"We'll be in Glens Falls soon," Beau says. Mimi smiles. Rudi opens his eyes.

"I seemed to doze for just a moment," he begins to dictate to Mimi, "and could see the faces of several people I loved the deepest. A great warmth filled me and positive energy moved down my brain to my heart and my sex organs..."

The clouds thicken. In one moment, the clear sky has given way to dark layers of fog that swallow the plane. I can't see the moon, the Hudson, remnants of the setting sun. The sky has become a battleground for dragons, the thick fog a backdrop for whirling, dreamlike things created at the genesis of time.

"Although it has been a few minutes since the experience took place," Rudi continues to dictate, "I feel completely renewed. It is exciting to see how these changes have the capacity to reflect a higher creativity. I am deeply looking forward to teaching the class tonight."

As I look out the plane's window into the black night and dark clouds, I can barely see a thousand feet in front of me. The fog and my thoughts seem to drift together into the far precincts of a void. My vision is blindsided by fear of a potentially dangerous future staring at me from the other side of the windshield. I've been told that great spiritual masters are prophetic. Rudi often says energy frequency emanating from a person gives insight into their future. I don't know. At the moment, I can't even see the ground.

There was a time when I forgot about the past and the future, when I baked in the late morning summer's sun that warmed Rudi's Big Indian ashram. I dragged tree trunks down the side of a mountain — my t–shirt soaked with sweat, my arms and hands scratched and bleeding, I was working to clear the slope and to plant an apple orchard. Rudi walked barefoot and bare–chested up the hill. I followed him. My body ached and I wanted to lie down and forget about apples and orchards; I followed him up and down and down and up the mountain's slope, dragging dead trees in his wake, piling them on a fire, chanting *"Om Namah Sivaya"* to myself, listening to my inner voice echo the sounds of a silent Hindu mantra. The fire crackled in the noonday sun. It spit and belched orange, yellow and blue flames, and devoured log after log, transforming them into ashes and dust. *"Sri Ram, Jai Ram,"* I chanted to myself...an apple orchard on each hill...four to five years till we pick the first fruit...planning...*"Jai Ram, Om."* Where will I be in five years...? Maybe I'll still be planning...?

Does it really matter? I thought. My future begins here on this mountain — a future of many moments linked together by a chain of mindless events that stretch the perimeters of time — a future that doesn't exist without this moment; and me, fool that I am, who can't live in the present because I spend all my time dwelling on yesterdays and tomorrows. My mind is a nonstop continuum that drifts from the past to the future. It has a shifting, changing, fearful, guilt–ridden vision of the world — unstable and unholy, it's linked to illusion and created from threads of fear and unhappiness that I foolishly substitute for reality. All I want is yesterday and tomorrow to dissolve into the present. Then there'll be nothing to fear and nothing to be guilty about. Why can't I live in the moment? Why can't I enjoy the gift of my life?

Rudi once asked me to clean a showcase in his store. I was tired and spent more time resisting the chore then actually doing it. He chastised me because I did a half–assed job, and I remember being angry and hurt and wanting to run away.

"Would you clean it like that in your own home?" he said to me. "If you volunteer to do something, do it well. Invest yourself in it. Love what you are doing. Even the smallest acts are an expression of God's energy working through you. How else do you get free? To serve is to uplift the earth and to bring higher consciousness to whatever you do."

"But it's just a showcase," I mumbled.

"I don't give a damn if it's a tile in the bathroom. It's not a showcase, Stuart. It's your life and stop crapping it up."

I picked up the rag and cleaner, and for two hours, polished the showcase until it shone.

I had grown tired of being a court jester living an unconscious life at the eye of a hurricane, I think. I once again look out the plane window at darkening clouds. I grew tired of being angry, resentful, and unhappy... so dragging trees down a mountain slope wasn't so bad after all, and Rudi scolding me wasn't so bad...I've learned that one moment gives birth to the next, that fire, ashes, dust, sweat and burning trees and brush are simply the present giving birth to the future. One day, I'll sit beneath a mature tree in the orchard and eat a ripe apple. A string of moments will take me there…a cycle will fulfill itself.

A slight breeze rippled the uncut grass at the base of the slope and the noonday sun was nothing short of oppressive. A perfect day for fishing, I thought as I threw another tree trunk into the fire.

"Nature's serene setting doesn't lessen human anxiety," Rudi said as we walked back up the slope. "People bring their craziness out to pasture, not realizing that the 'simple life' is more in the minds of men than in daily living. Years of inner work teach us to be simple. No environment can act as a substitute for the mastery of self; no environment can cure ego sickness. A human being is not an orchid that needs to live in a special hothouse." He picked up some dead branches and gathered them in his arms and with a smile on his face, he said, "The Japanese Zen painter often creates a masterpiece when he draws a single line. His simplicity is, in truth, the product of many years of meditation and study. He has silenced his mind and emotions and every line he draws is a spontaneous expression of the moment. Years of spiritual study teach this. A particular environment might relax us for a few hours, but truly simple souls bring light and love and consciousness to every place and situation."

I stopped for a moment and studied a butterfly on a lotus blossom floating in a pond, and I listened to the drone of a bee winging its way from flower to flower. The sky's clear blue extended to the infinite; the mountains seemed to breathe, and the valley pulsated. If only my mind would shut up, if only I could stop its rasping voice and give myself a moment's peace.

"Conflict is woven into the earth's fabric," Rudi said as we stood at the base of the mountain's slope. "It's guaranteed that a positive experience will be followed by a negative one. They trail each other around like night and day. But positive and negative are the same energy in different costumes. Both teach us how to get to God. Perhaps the most important lesson I have ever learned is how to transform my tension into a life–giving force and to finally accept that I attract to myself exactly what I give off. If I can't forgive someone else, how can they forgive me? It makes me smile, Stuart, to think it's a miracle that anyone lives through a day. People's tensions are so acute that it deadens them to reality."

What about ashrams and spiritual schools, I thought. I threw dead branches into the fire and watched them crackle and burn until they turned to ashes. Most of these schools are over–crowded with people's emotional and mental baggage, with egos running wild through meditation rooms and corridors, with silence trips, food trips and self–righteous spiritual trips, with men and women and children tripping over each other's ideas, never taking a moment to listen to the voice of God. It's easy to point to someone else's problems and difficult to fathom our own. It's easy to say, "I forgive them," but more difficult to find forgiveness for the thousands of transgressions each of us makes in the course of a lifetime. When I think of Shakespeare's King Lear leading blind Gloucester through torrential rains at the edge of the White Cliffs of Dover, I think of the blind child in all of us being led through life by the false wisdom of madmen. We're like lost sheep running in and out of a pen that's tainted by the human mind's short–sighted vision. The mad lead the blind through fog and rain to chasms filled with lost souls. But, somewhere there's got to be love, somewhere, there's got to be a place where life's turbulent waters get calm and I can live each day with an open heart.

"But why all the fighting?" I asked Rudi. "Why can't people live together in harmony? It's an ashram, for God's sake, a spiritual school."

"They're people, aren't they?" He laughed as he dragged another tree trunk down the slope, "and people by their very nature are crazy. They pee all over paradise."

"But you still work with them."

"With the God in them," he answered, "with the seed of life that needs soil and water and a place to grow. It doesn't matter why they come or how crazy they are. The only important thing is that they want a spiritual life. The rest will take care of itself. The *shakti* can heal almost any condition. I've met hundreds of people who eat the right foods, dress in Aquarian Age clothes, smell from incense, say the right words, but it's almost impossible to find among them a person with joy in his or her heart, with love and compassion — someone who takes full responsibility for their life — in a word, a human being. Once we learn how to do this, the rest is easy.

"The important thing, Stuart, is who'll be doing our work twenty years from now — you, me, a few others. The rest will receive a little now and they'll give a little. Then they'll disappear into the great yawn of life. Many years ago, I discovered that I was born to serve God, not people. People change. One minute they love you, the next, they turn on you. The human mind and heart are fragile and full of conflict. They're never at peace, never in balance. They say, 'For many are called but few are chosen.' This is a great truth. Though many people covet a spiritual life, few are willing to work to get it. You've got to be willing to take a coal chisel and chip your way through a mountain. Most people refuse to spend their entire lives chipping away at themselves. Most people are not ready for deep spiritual work, so the universe gives them thousands of lifetimes to become ready. It's a matter of evolution. When you truly need God you work your ass off to get to Him."

"So why teach?"

"Because it's the last step in the evolutionary process. You don't choose to teach. It's an outgrowth of years of inner work — a way of being used by God in this world. At best, a teacher is a servant. He serves God and he serves the need his students have for a spiritual life and inner growth. A vehicle for Higher Creative Energy, he channels a life–giving force called *shakti* that uplifts the consciousness of people around him. His students reflect his own limitations and they clearly show him the work he's got to do on himself in order to attain enlightenment. If he doesn't give his teachings away, they congest him and instantly become a powerful limitation. A teacher that's incapable of surrendering his position as a teacher, will substitute ego, intellect, and personality for spirit, and use them to solidify his position on earth. He becomes a limitation for everyone around him. If he doesn't love his students and forgive them their lack of consciousness, how are they going to learn to forgive themselves?"

Billions of people live on earth and almost all of them will one day be forgotten, I muse. Rudi's hand squeezes mine and I turn to him. We smile at each other. He closes his eyes and tries to sleep. Once more, I look into the black sky with patches of cloud bouncing off our plane and think that one day I'll be forgotten too. I'll be just a note recorded in a cosmic ledger and filed in a wastepaper basket woven from the threads of time. Big Indian will be forgotten. Beau and Mimi and Rudi will all be forgotten. The truth of the matter is that I can barely remember what I had for breakfast this morning or to whom I first spoke today. Why is it important to be remembered? Why is it important to be different than most people that disappear in the annals of time?

"Every person who's been in my life has helped me get closer to God," Rudi said as we stopped for a moment on the Big Indian ashram mountain slope to rest. "I love them and I'm grateful to them; those that are with me today and those I'll probably never see again." The lunch bell rang and we walked to the dining hall. "We never know how God comes to us," Rudi continued talking. "He's a master quick–change artist with thousands of costumes and masks. He has myriad ways of teaching us and most of them make no sense. The first thing we learn is that it's impossible to approach Infinite Energy with all of our preconceptions. The reason for this is simple: one moment we feel loved, and the next it feels like our suffering is beyond endurance. Gurus are also a little like that. They don't fit into a box. You love them and hate them and never quite know what will come next. Their very presence forces a disciple to open inside and receive spiritual energy."

How true! I think, laughing to myself, and remembering how one moment I'd love Rudi, and the next, I'd be jealous, angry, and running out the door. I wondered how it was possible to hate the person I loved the most in the world, the person who'd done more for me than any other living being. The silent shout of "Rudi Rudi" always filled me as I ran headlong into a mental cul-de-sac. I knew that he was my last chance to get to God; I knew that I'd have to surrender in greater depth, that I couldn't run away anymore, that I'd have to toe-to-toe it with my own craziness. I resented surrender. I resented my stupidity, my insecurity, my inability to function, but mostly I resented feeling like a schmuck all the time, not knowing how Rudi could love such a schmuck, not knowing if I'd ever crawl out of my backward condition.

"We always fight with the people we love the most," Rudi said as we walked on the ashram grounds toward the large, old hotel that acted as dining hall and lodging. We crossed a plank bridge spanning a stream gurgling down the mountainside and walked along a blacktop country road that wound past the hotel and bridge to a dead end half a mile uphill. The ashram nestled in a valley surrounded by low-lying mountains — the perfect getaway for a bunch of New York City yogis needing weekends of meditation, work, and country air.

"Our parents are number one on our hit lists," Rudi continued talking as we walked to the dining hall. "We blame them for every bullshit thing they did to us. We forget that they're just human beings struggling with their own lives and limitations. People hold on to hurts inflicted in childhood and never let go. They never trust again and find themselves stuck in infantile mud — living like petrified trees in a forest. If we don't forgive our parents, who is going to forgive us? Does it really matter what someone did to us when we were two years-old? No! There's not a soul in the world that gives a shit except the person shouldering tons of guilt. We've become adept at using the past to stunt emotional and mental growth and remain neurotic children in a so-called adult world. Our parents are not gods! They're humans — imperfect, emotionally blind, afraid, and battling to survive. We place them on pedestals and tear them down because they don't live up to our ideas of perfection. Yet, they're still our parents. They gave birth to us. If we don't love them, we'll never be free.

"When I was two years-old, my mother, in a fit of rage, threw me down a flight of steps and cracked open my head. I spent months in a hospital. I mean, a rational person doesn't throw a two year-old child down a flight of steps. Acts like that are committed in moments of insanity. First, she tried to kill me, then she spent months nursing me back to health. After years of struggling with this, I learned to forgive her. I came to realize that if I don't forgive her, how would she ever forgive herself? It's the quickest way to a truce. I'm the one having a spiritual life. I'm the one who's supposed to be the more conscious person. I've got to make up the difference. I can't hold onto a past that'll destroy every effort I make to grow and change. She's my mother and I've got to love her. I've got to do it for myself, for my own life, for my own happiness. If not, my heart will ache for the rest of my life."

The lunch bell rang a second time.

If I'm the problem, I must be the solution, I thought. Rudi and I sat for a moment on the ashram lawn before entering the dining hall. But I don't know how to free myself from myself; I don't know how long it takes to resolve things.

I delighted in the one o'clock sun and in breezes sifting through tall grass, in the chants of crickets and frogs and the voices of people that had gathered near the dining hall. I put my arm around Rudi and said, "Thank you".

"You're learning," he said. "You're my son, you know, and you're learning the ways of God."

The ways of God and the ways of man, crowded on a small planet and jockeying for position, I think. The plane continues to fly through thick clouds. I can't see the earth or the sky. How do I repay someone who's saved my life, who's teaching me the ways of God? No gift or service is enough, not clearing mountain slopes, roofing houses, painting fire escapes, cleaning toilets, refrigerators and sinks, preparing breakfast for twenty people each morning; nothing is enough. I don't know what else to do. All that's left is total surrender to God, and perhaps, someday, I'll be able to do the same for another person. Perhaps, someday...

"Mediocrity is instant death," Rudi said as we entered the Big Indian ashram dining hall, "yet people strive for it like it's some kind of panacea — a security that'll protect them from life's dangers. Status quo turns creative energy into a disease–infested puddle of water that attracts the lowest levels of life. A brook flows down a mountain. Anyone can drink from its waters. Dam it up, make a pond, puddle or lake, and the water gets polluted. Mosquitoes swarm and bacteria and algae grow in it. If you drink the water, it'll kill you."

"I didn't expect this," Beau says to himself.

He snaps me out of my reverie. The fog's density has increased to where I can't see ten feet in front of me. Grey and black clouds have come from nowhere. They're whirling about, consuming me, and sucking the power out of my belly. Up. Down. Vertigo. Beau fidgets with the instrument panel. He seems unsure of himself.

I close my eyes, and in my mind's eye, I see seventy–five apple trees on a hill, each with two giant apples; I see thousands of bottles of apple juice and apple sauce covering a five–acre lawn, and a fire leaping through clouds and darkness, filling the sky with an orange, yellow, and red glow. The plane flies just above the conflagration. I see Rudi sitting naked and in full lotus in a burial ground–like meadow of charred grass. Two grinning skeletons dance around him. A crow is perched in his lap. "They told me I'd die when I was thirty–one," he says. "I gave up my school and my business and left New York, planning never to return. I headed for New Zealand by way of India and wound up in the village of Ganeshpuri where a friend of mine told me a great Hindu saint lived. 'It's only a three–hour drive from Bombay,' my friend said. 'You must meet Swami Nityananda. He is truly an enlightened being. He'll help you in your spiritual search.'"

The next morning, Rudi rose early, met his friend, and they drove to the village. The dusty Indian road passed through small town after small town. Cows slept at the center of the road, and live and dead water buffalo littered the streets and pastures. In one village, a dead water buffalo was in the process of being eaten by an army of buzzards, and naked *saddhus* strolled leisurely down the dusty street. Pedestrians, bicycles, motor scooters, carts drawn by horses or water buffalo, elephants, dogs, cats, cows, Brahman bulls, hundreds of women with large water pots on their heads, cars, taxis and trucks decorated with images of gods, all vied for a position on the road. People were working in the fields gathering dry cow patties for building huts, and everywhere you looked there stood temples and shrines for local gods and goddesses worshipped by the predominantly Hindu population. It was a visual feast. He loved every moment of it.

The head teacher at the New York Gurdjieff Institute had read Rudi's astrological chart and told him that he would die at age thirty–one. He suggested that Rudi should go to New Zealand to study with a *Subud* master. Rudi checked his reading with other psychics and got variations of the same theme.

"But no one mentioned Swami Nityananda to me, no one told me that this guru's *shakti* would disassemble me piece by piece and transport me into a deep spiritual trance. It was like being hit by a laser beam. When I came out of the trance, I immediately knew that I had found my spiritual master. Swami Nityananda had given birth to me."

No one had ever told him that Nityananda would change the fear of death into life–affirming energy and a new level of consciousness; no one ever told him that this swami would enter his heart.

"Every night," Rudi said, "I would sleep with his astral being lying next to me and see my hands transform themselves into Swami Nityananda's hands. One day, while in the gardens outside my hotel in Delhi, his soul–force came to me. It walked by my side and told me that my true work is in service of God. I had met Babaji only once in the flesh. A year later, when I returned to Ganeshpuri and discovered that he'd taken his *samadhi*, that he'd gone to be with God, I never felt any loss. You see Swami Nityananda lives in my heart. He's always with me.

"I want to die and be reborn every day till I leave the world; I want to continue surrendering to my own nothingness. But don't forget, Stuart, it takes at least seven years from the time you meet your teacher to make a permanent commitment to a spiritual life."

The dark and whirling fog, I think. No place to put my feet down... only seven difficult years to test my desire to be free...

"We use time cheaply," Rudi once said to me while we were sitting together in his antique store. "We use it as if we had forever to live. Then we're forty, fifty or sixty years old and we wonder what happened. Where'd our lives go? The *chakra* system has atrophied to a point almost beyond redemption. Time is a great Bodhisattva that gives us eternity to attain enlightenment. We ride its merry–go–round through illusion after illusion, through lifetime after lifetime, until our suffering drives us to God. Time has more patience than I do. It can put up with people's bullshit forever.

"Our work isn't for everyone," he went on. "But those who survive seven years or ten years or twenty years of it, they'll find the hidden treasure. They're the people in whom I've got to invest my energy."

It took me nine years to find Rudi. From the moment my father died when I was sixteen to the day I walked into Rudi's antique store, nine years in which I danced a mad spiritual dance that brought me to the point of death or insanity. I desperately wanted God. I chanted, prayed, devised meditation practices for myself, smoked marijuana and took LSD till my brain bled with visions. I climbed a self–constructed ladder to a pastel cloud on which gods and demigods voiced cosmic messages to a deaf seeker. I shirked responsibility and believed work anathema to sensible living — a prison for fools and slaves. I lived on the edge of a flat planet where multi-armed demons lured me into a sea of madness. I spoke to no one for months at a time and became a recluse in the heart of New York City — an anchorite of sorts, silently screaming at the heavens, the rooftops, the blank faces on the streets, and saying to myself, "No one and nothing gives a shit about your inner revolution." Then I thought, who cares? I don't really give a damn about the tormented faces I see in the streets, about an uncaring God, about my thoughts bouncing off New York City buildings.

I continued to wander in a wilderness of my own creation. No one but I could enter it. No one could even get near me. I had created my own version of God and believed, for many years, that I knew all the answers. I'd stroll hand in hand with fear through Central Park, down Fifth Avenue, through Greenwich Village, and lived in awe of a vast, uncharted, inner world of mind and spirit.

"Did you ever feel like a roach?" I once asked a stranger on a street. "You know, crawling in and out of holes, living on dust and grime, always hunting and being hunted, always afraid."

"No," he said, and walked nervously away from me. He stopped for a moment, looked at me, shrugged his shoulders and disappeared around a corner.

Nothing made sense to me when I was sixteen years-old. Not that it makes sense now, but at sixteen I thought that I knew something about life. Sixteen should be a time to play; it should be a time to grow up and begin to make sense of things, but sense and nonsense shattered my thoughts when I was told, while sunbathing in Miami Beach, that my father was dying. Nobody had taught me about death and dying. Fathers weren't supposed to die. At least mine wasn't. Other people's fathers did die all the time, but that was outside the safe and sheltered world of sixteen year-old Stuart vacationing in Miami Beach.

My mother, sister and I flew back to New York City to find my fever-racked father suffering from acute colitis. He continued to move in and out of a conscious state. He shivered for ten straight days until there was barely anything left of him. Then his breathing stopped and a doctor pronounced him dead. He didn't know me, and I realized I didn't know him either. I hid behind a curtain of my own fear. I didn't want to come out. Nothing made sense. Not my life, not his death...nothing at all.

He's a simple man, I thought, modest in his needs, loving, hard-working, a supporter of his family, and yet, I couldn't remember one important conversation I ever had with him; I couldn't remember one declaration of love. Forty–nine years of busting his ass…for what…for a malfunctioning colon to take it all away? So his helpless son can stand by and watch the father he never knew leave this world? Again, I asked myself: "For what?" I didn't know. I still don't know. I wondered if ten days were all there was to life. In those ten days, I learned about my father. I watched him burn until he could burn no more, and I watched him come out of a coma a few hours before his death. He lovingly took my hand, gazed at me and said, "Stuart."

"You know me?" I asked him. I sat in a chair next to his bed. Tears were in my eyes.

"Yes," he replied.

An otherworldly glow filled the room.

"Yes," he said again.

Then he squeezed my hand. His deep, black eyes were two bottomless pools. They were sad, joyful, loving, and eternal. They swept me into their spiritual radiance.

He's been with God, I thought, and everything's all right. I mean, to live is all right and to die is all right. He's been with God and he's surrendered everything to Him.

"I love you," I said.

He smiled and said that he loved me too, that he was happy at last and at peace with himself. He died three hours later.

After years of meditation practice, I realized that my father, in his last moments, had become my first spiritual teacher. He changed the course of my life and thrust me into the arms of Rudi.

After his death, I rebelled against family, friends, school, and all institutions. I convinced myself that suffering was the common denominator of the human race. But I never forgot the clear light in my father's eyes. I never forgot that sense of peace in the hospital room. I asked myself why he had to wait forty–nine years to find God, why inner peace came to him the last three hours of his life, why he didn't find it ten years sooner and share it with people he loved.

A frightened child is a lost child no matter how old he is; a frightened child stops at nothing to hide his fear. He lies awake all night and sobs under his breath. He believes no one truly understands his fear. He'll cry until he exhausts himself and stamp his foot until it hurts. A frightened child is often an active child busying himself to cover his fear. He can't tolerate other people's pain, yet he'll torment them, and sometimes he finds comfort in other people's suffering. A frightened child is a lonely child wandering by himself outside of the gates of Eden. He's a child that also wanders through thousands of lost memories. A frightened child finally grows up when his pain becomes unbearable, when he runs out of excuses and secret hiding places, when he's tired of being pulled by the undertow of life's ocean. His choices become simple: God or suicide, life or death, joy or fear. I know about frightened children. For ten years I looked for ways to appease my fear in the nooks and crannies of Spiritual America. I pleaded with God to show me a path; I fought with myself and I tried to get answers from anyone who'd listen. Then I met Rudi. As I left his antique store on that first day, he had a beatific smile on his face, and the light that surrounded him was no different than the light I saw in my father's hospital room the day he died.

I've spent most of my life listening to my thoughts, and these thoughts deafened me to the songs of birds, and to the words of other people. I discovered that one hour of an active mind is more exhausting than a day of hard physical labor. I've heard Rudi teach that the whole universe is within each of us. Then why can't I hear it? Why is there so much excess noise? Why does my mind keep coming apart?

My thoughts often take me on a boat that sails turbulent waters between heaven and hell. Along the way are gurus, swamis, *rishis, nagababas,* all of them wise men dressed in orange robes, white *kurtas,* purple caftans, wise men wearing beards, *malas* and sandals — all freshly arrived from the East. Flower children dance naked in their presence. They welcome these teachers as voices of enlightenment in the Aquarian Age. These wise men have come to the West to remind us of love, joy, and spirituality. The flower children eat pecks of mushrooms. They smoke bales of peyote, hashish, marijuana, and they down LSD like aspirin. They fuck and march and protest and riot and throw dust in the eyes of their parents — a generation of drop-outs, rebels, long-hairs and saints, living like wind-up toys suspended in a void.

How many times did I say to myself, "I'm a flower child…I'm certain God and His angels have blessed us…His outcast bohemians?"

I'd listen to bright-eyed swamis mouthing "Love, Peace and Eat Vegetable" mantras; bright-eyed swamis fresh from remote caves in the Himalayas who'd recite excerpts from the *Bhagavad Gita* to kids from the Bronx, swamis with no sense of what it takes to survive a New York City day. I would back away, become reclusive, smoke a joint, chant at a local temple, have dinner at a macrobiotic restaurant and congratulate myself on walking the spiritual path. It was all I knew…all I understood.

I squeeze Rudi's hand and look at him sitting in the rear seat of the airplane. He was the most irreverent person I'd ever met. At the same time, he was a living expression God's spirit on earth — a highly-conscious being who spent his life working day and night to serve Higher Energy in the Universe. He once told me that if I'm pure inside, I can eat shit and it will turn to gold; that in India, I could sit and chant and meditate for twenty years, and after all that time, only my ass would grow; that it would take at least a half-dozen incarnations to learn what swami so-and-such had to teach; that foundation and technique were essential to spiritual practice; that I've got to learn to fix myself the same way a mechanic learns to fix a car.

"Human beings are mostly broken-down machines that need fixing," he said one afternoon when we were in a pizza parlor getting a slice. He went on to tell me that celibate holy men must've exhausted their sex lives in their last incarnation. In his life, he had met thousands of so-called spiritual people and very few human beings.

"All people want is to love and be loved," he said after we finished our slices of pizza. "Even the most horrible crime is committed by someone trying to touch the world."

"The inability of students," Rudi continues to dictate to Mimi, "and teachers to do what they are given is what creates problems for them. They wander through basic experience, not having the ability to sustain any simple effort. But this is precisely the process that builds a strong foundation, which supports the whole structure."

"Was there a forecast of fog?" I ask Beau.

"No. We'll be out of it in a few minutes."

I don't know if he's telling me the truth or telling me to back off and not bother him. But a few minutes isn't such a long time when you think that it takes an hour to fly from Teeterboro to Glens Falls. It's gonna be cold out, I mean, I'm wearing a spring jacket and Glens Falls is a hundred-some odd miles north of the city, and New York City's always fifteen degrees warmer than anywhere upstate.

It's probably a short run from the airplane to the terminal. A little cold won't kill me. But I've never seen fog like this. Yet pilots fly in fog all the time. Their instruments make it possible to land a plane without seeing the runway.

"We're experts at everyone else's problems but our own," Rudi once said in a lecture at Big Indian. "The self is a great mystery to us. It's the gateway to the unknown and the unknown is the wellspring of all creative energy. What we understand about life can fit into a shot glass. The rest is mysterious. It's a smorgasbord of untasted delights, a table set for our enjoyment. If we're not afraid of living and dying, then we can taste every dish on the table. When we finally die, there's nothing to come back to earth for."

But human tension is very hard to digest whether it's served on a gourmet platter or like junk food, I think. It tears apart our digestive systems and fries our brains. It's unmanageable, scary — an intangible force that cripples people before they get old.

"It's easy to help other people," Rudi went on. "The hard thing is helping ourselves; it's hard to use our tension to grow spiritually. Instead we use it to pound those around us into pulp."

I wonder if the mountain I climb inside myself is the same mountain worshipped by the ancients; I wonder if they believed in uphill struggles to find God, if they saw human beings as vast landfills full of physical and psychological waste, and if their cairns, pyramids and *stupas* were nothing more than altars commemorating pollution–free consciousness. There are mountains at the center of the universe, at the ends of the earth, below oceans, and in the cosmos; there's Mount Meru, Mount Olympus, Ararat, Kailash, Abu, and Sinai; there's the Sermon on the Mount and the mountain Sisyphus climbs and re–climbs, and scores of other mountains that appear and reappear in every religious book. Many are sources of sacred rivers that cultivate the earth. People bathe in these rivers and pray to them, and fervently offer them the ashes of their dead. I often find myself a quarter way up an inner mountain created from excess psychological shit, and though each step I take exhausts me, I never stop trying to reach its peak. The very struggle makes me strong and helps me to free myself from myself.

"We don't know how wounded we are until we begin to heal ourselves," Rudi said in one of his lectures. "The unconscious self is a Pandora's box filled with pain — a nest of seething asp–like wounds that won't heal until we effectively change inside ourselves, wounds that destroy mind, body and spirit, that find their way into the blood stream, joints, muscles, heart and inner organs, and plunder the body of its vital resources, wounds that disembowel us, that make us sexually impotent. We accept sickness as the natural outgrowth of age and seek help from physicians who prescribe medicines to cure the symptoms not the causes. A lifetime of tension breaks down the body. We forget the first maxim of medicine: 'physician heal thyself' or 'patient take care of thyself'. A newborn child is delicious, sweet, filled with nothing but joy, love, and happiness, yet most people, before they die, are dried up, rotten and arthritic specimens of life, disgusting and smelling of death and putrefaction."

"Hello! Hello!" Beau is whispering into the radio.

"Spiritual work reverses the aging process," Rudi continues in my thoughts. "As the body gets older, the inner self gets younger and we radiate childlike essence and spontaneity. We're not afraid to improvise with life."

"Hello!" Beau whispers again.

"Night cometh" and goeth through fog and eddies of cloud and wind circling the plane, I think. A black sky made blacker by dark thoughts and memories; a primal force reaching into my soul and shaking loose past attachments; a sky the color of liquid ink; a plane moving forever forward. I can't see ten feet out the front window.

"It's always easier to feed our system from the same stream by deepening and lengthening the amount of time given to an exercise than to look for a new source," Rudi dictates to Mimi. "Involved and dramatic methods allow us to lose the basic discipline from which we receive our strength. We must check any deviation from our basic effort, since it is that effort that perpetuates the line of energy, that makes for elasticity as well as extraordinary deep strength."

"I'm afraid of vertigo," Beau whispers to me. "I've got to see the ground." The plane's altitude drops to eight thousand feet. Beau fidgets nervously with the instrument panel.

"How low?" I ask him. He doesn't answer. His entire concentration is focused on flying. I feel Rudi's hand in mine and turn to him and smile. He returns my smile. His presence comforts me. It makes me feel that everything is all right.

I close my eyes, take a deep breath, and try to relax. My mind begins to drift. It's dark out I think, and the night is a little more mysterious than the day, especially when I can't see ten feet in front of my nose. The night has come before its time and sweeps me into the unknown. But I have no fear. I have Rudi in my heart. What can happen?

"I'm a technician," he once said about himself in the living room of his apartment. "I teach the mechanics of spiritual work. Meditation is nothing more than a craft that uses the mind and breath as tools to open *chakras. Chakras* are psychic muscles that are connected directly to the force of Higher Creative Energy. If we open the *chakras,* and strengthen them, we can draw cosmic energy to the earth, and use it in our daily lives. A fool leaves his spiritual life in a meditation room."

The night and fog dance to the drone of propeller wings and the rhythm of Beau's nervous hands; the night and fog come from nowhere and go to nowhere at 125 MPH. I chant to myself, *"Sri Ram, Jai Ram, Jai Ram, Ram Om."* I look for *Siva* riding his bull on a cloud. I look into the fog and think that somewhere on the other side of all this is a glimpse of God.

"To me, the *chakra* system is no more mysterious than the digestive system, respiratory system or circulatory system," Rudi once said. "It is as essential to my life as breathing. I never take it for granted. I've built a bridge connecting an awakened *chakra* system with the outer world. The real guru is life in all its infinite manifestations.

"Without foundation, we're like tumbleweeds bouncing off of picket fences. Every plant and tree has a root system. Animals nest to birth their young, but people drift through life..."

My thoughts drift into memory. There's pre–Rudi and Rudi. Pre–Rudi dredges up visions of seedy apartments and hotel rooms in countries all over the world. It dredges up drugged–out forays into the heart of the Buddha, loneliness and despair, and the fear of spending my life in a sanitarium. I lived like a thousand–foot flower wilting for lack of water. Now, at least, I'm beginning to see possibilities of serving God in the world.

I once prided myself on being an angry young man, until a cautionary inner voice said to me, "There's no sense trying to tear apart political and social structures. They're too dense, cryptic...too insulated. They're like bureaucratic hydras that replace departments, wings, buildings, embassies and employees without any effort. One day, it will all become a dim memory in the minds of those who lived through the sixties. The deeds of revolutionaries will be lauded in PBS documentary films that a handful of people will watch. The rest of the world will be too busy making ends meet. 'Goin' down to D.C. town...tear it down...tear it down...' I wanted to see the Buddha rise from ashes and embrace the sun. 'Goin' down to DC town...' But it doesn't work that way. It never does.' I tried to see God in eddies of smoke rising from empty dirt lots. Then I discovered that all I really wanted was to breathe fresh air and to get a clearer vision of God.

On one political protest march, a friend said to me: "They'll get us. They'll stick tubes in our ears, make lampshades of our skin, drain our blood, pluck out our pubic hairs. Then they'll forget about us. They'll leave us to dry in the sun or tie us to a rock and let vultures feed on our livers."

'Goin' down to D.C. town,' I thought, 'where the Buddha rises from ashes and embraces the sun…'

"We attract to ourselves exactly what we give off," Rudi once said to me in a Chinatown restaurant, "and a strong *chakra* system radiates balance, love, serenity, and the strength to take full responsibility for our lives. The trick is to live in the world and outside of it at exactly the same time. The trick is to not be trapped by anything. It's not what you have, but whether what you have has you. There's a story I remember hearing in India about a *sanyasin* who sat for twenty years in profound meditation beneath a tree. He had taken vows of poverty and possessed only a loincloth and a begging bowl. One day, he decided to leave his spot beneath the tree. He might have had to go to the bathroom or something. But when he returned to the tree, he found another *sanyasin* sitting there. Without a thought, he beat the holy man with a stick, cursed him, chased him away, and once again sat beneath his tree where he continued to meditate for another twenty years."

When we finished eating and walked from Chinatown to his house on Tenth Street, as always, he felt talkative and imparted wisdom to his grateful student. It was a cold winter's night and the streets were empty, but the twenty-degree weather didn't affect my ability to listen.

"Years ago," he said, "I learned that society's social and economic fabric is my best protection. Whatever money I earn and success I have serve a singular purpose, and that's to support my spiritual life. It's the best disguise because it gives me the freedom to live in the world and outside the world at exactly the same time. We don't live in an *'either/or'* world, but in an all-inclusive world in which nothing conflicts with anything else. Only the mind creates polarity. Once we quiet its noise box, the outer world's mirror image of ourselves reflects greater harmony."

Yes! Yes! My love! I thought, laughing. Someday my mind will stop its chitchat. Someday I will just disappear. You'll look up in the sky and see me there — a light flickering in the heavens. I can easily forget the paint I threw on government walls, the love songs I sang with other hippies in Central Park. Was it all for nothing? — just a memory of another time.

"The purpose of money and power is to give life," he said. We were walking north on Mulberry Street past brightly-lit Italian restaurants on either side of us. "Most people forget this and money becomes a sacred goal that sucks the vital juices out of them. They dry up spiritually. They burn out. They get heart conditions and cancer and many other diseases that come when the obsession for money controls every action. I'm not denigrating success in life. I think it's very important if for no other reason than we have to free ourselves from society's sick obsession with money. It's important because we can't free ourselves from things we don't have. We have to realize that wealth doesn't guarantee happiness and, too often, we get lost in a financial whirlwind that ultimately takes us to the grave. We're eaten alive by the sick thought that money is the new God, and the more of it we accumulate, the more important our position is on earth. No one gets to God unless they've learned to surrender their position on earth. Money has a singular purpose, and that's to nurture the people we love. If we recognize that it's just energy, and if we realize that energy, when manifesting on earth, has both positive and negative qualities, we can transform our obsession with making money into a life–giving force. I use it to support my spiritual work. Spent wisely, it makes room for people to study with me. Can there be any greater reward in my life than helping someone find his or her path to God? When I see lost and unhappy people learn to open their hearts and be grateful, it's a greater reward for me than reaping billions of dollars. This isn't philanthropic work that requires tax deductions and, in almost every case, is nothing more than a half–assed attempt to promote one's ego or buy one's way into heaven. Money is just energy. Used consciously, it gives life, and used unconsciously, it sucks the vital juices out of everyone. It never brings happiness and always gives a false sense of security. We try to escape the inevitable by burying our self in over–zealous ambition."

Someday I'll talk to God about my financial problems, I think, with a smile on my face while looking out of the plane window; and at some point the fog will disappear and we'll land in Glens Falls.

"No one knows a thing about life, but it's impossible to find a person who'll admit it," Rudi said as we crossed Houston Street. "The past trails us around like a late–afternoon shadow. Though it has no substance, it still keeps us a prisoner of our mistakes. The mind recreates the past from dimly–lit memories of the way things were, twisting and turning everything to suit its own purposes, never focusing on things with clarity of perception. If we live a vital, healthy life filled with spiritual consciousness, the past falls away like an appendage. We discover that the future, present and past exist in the moment, and the moment is the all–inclusive factor of human existence. The present doesn't give a shit about the past. It has no time. It's too busy living its own soap opera, not realizing that today's soap opera becomes a piece of driftwood floating in memory. People are very serious about their slapstick behavior. They're like toads wearing spectacles, bloated, bubbling, and trying to stay out of the rain. It's more fun watching them than an Our Gang comedy movie. They distort issues, elevate or depress them according to self–interest, blame their troubles on dummy–like images in the hands of political and economic ventriloquists. Everyone's guessing, but no one will admit it; everyone's competing for five seconds in the limelight."

Everyone's groping in his personal fog, I think, as I open my eyes and stare at the black pit now engulfing our plane. Transcendental visions are the insights of fools and visionaries. Practical people have no time for stuff like that. Their day ends at five o'clock: a few drinks, dinner, TV, the wife, kids, sleep, up again, and off to work. Day after day, year after year – that's how my father died…that's how my father died…that's how the world ends…that's how I will turn to ash…how my heart and head will go blank. How many times, in dreams, have I angrily shaken my father and asked why it took forty–nine years for him to find God...

"In a class, years ago, a bone cracked in my forehead," Rudi said. We were walking north on the Bowery past flophouses and homeless men and women sleeping on the streets. "You could hear the pop during the meditation. A phoenix bird flew out of my third eye and circled the room. Look at my forehead, Stuart." He pointed to indentations directly above the eyebrows. "You can see the phoenix's wings there. They extend from the center of my forehead to the crown of my head. They're a sign of rebirth, of a continuous regeneration of life and spiritual energy." We stopped walking for a moment, and he put my hand on his forehead. I could feel jolts of shakti flowing through my body. "We've got to look and listen for signs," he went on. "I remember, years ago, I pleaded for weeks with God for a sign. One day, while walking across a dirt lot, a jolt of energy went up my spine, knocked me unconscious, and paralyzed me. I woke up in a hospital bed feeling nothing but joy and gratitude. 'At least God heard me,' I thought, 'at least He gave me a sign.' The logic of spiritual energy transcends human understanding. You don't make deals with God. There's no dotted line, no guarantees. There's just daily work, growth, and acceptance of teachings as they come.

"Preconception limits people to a finite vision of the universe. It's a creation of the rational mind and the rational mind is a devious clip joint run by swindlers and thieves. It robs us of true creativity and limits us to a safe, well-insulated existence fenced in by human understanding. But there's just so much we can understand. At some point, we've got to shrug our shoulders, bow down, and defer to a Higher Force. No matter what answers come to me, no matter how intelligent my explanations, they're invalid minutes later. Life keeps changing its identity. Whatever I understand at one moment must be surrendered the next."

"Must I surrender even what works?" I asked him. We had just walked past Astor Place.

"Yes! Especially what works! If I don't deepen what works, regenerate it, and come to it in a new and vital way, 'what works' stagnates and becomes ineffective. I'll begin to take it for granted."

"I understand that," I said laughing.

"I'm sure," he answered with a smile.

"A guru is like a generator transmitting energy," he continued. "It doesn't matter if you agree or disagree with what he says or does. You don't even have to like him. What matters is that his teachings work for you, that they help you to grow and get closer to God. That's the only criteria. I studied thirteen years with a teacher I didn't like. I let him cut me into a thousand pieces, never judging, never questioning. I just took what I needed for my God-realization. People would ask me why I did it and I'd tell them, 'Baba's the only person I know who's strong enough to take me apart.'"

Rudi told me that India's a land of great saints and holy men, but you can chant and pray and kiss Baba's feet, and chant and pray until you're ninety, and still, when the teachings are passed on, an Indian is always next in line. A Westerner has got to fight every inch of the way.

Rudi sat at Baba's feet working his spiritual ass off to get shakti. He wanted Rudi to become a swami and put him through psychic test after psychic test. Rudi found himself playing hide-and-seek with Baba on the astral plane. At three in the morning Rudi would get up, chant and pray till eight, eat breakfast, work, chant and pray, have lunch, work and chant and pray, and drop into bed at the first trace of darkness. He'd eat rice three meals a day until rice reminded him of prison food.

Rudi didn't like being called swami. He thought it was a stupid title in the West, but Baba required it, and Rudi didn't want to argue with him. He was one of the first white people to be made a swami in India, but he didn't care. After Baba's intense psychic surgeries, after having his heart *chakra* cut open and Nityananda's soul placed in it, after chasing Baba around the Blue World — being a swami didn't seem so bad. Rudi needed Baba's help to sever all earthly attachments, and to strengthen his connection with God. It didn't matter the price; it didn't matter what he had to go through.

"You see, Baba's a great teacher," Rudi said to me one evening in his apartment. "He's also a strange and complex man...a magician of sorts. I've never tried to figure him out. I just open to him and take in his energy. What he does and doesn't do is his own business. He's not courting my favor, nor is he running for Miss America. He's a vehicle for God's energy — a cosmic tit. Years of studying with him have taught me to keep my mouth shut, to work deeply, and not to judge anything he says or does."

Baba came to America in the late summer of 1971. The ashram raised fifteen thousand dollars to help Baba make the trip and Rudi matched it. Baba arrived at Kennedy airport with an entourage of Indian holy men dressed in orange robes and women in colorful saris.

"Everybody loves my Baba. Oh! oh! oh!" Rudi sang as we waited. "There he is!"

The entourage passed through JFK as if centuries of time had come to a screeching halt. Hundreds of devotees greeted Baba, most never having seen him before, but all anxious to meet a great saint from the East — devotees carrying garlands of flowers, gifts, bouquets, and open hearts. Rudi bowed and kissed Baba's feet and Baba playfully slapped Rudi on the back. Baba was dressed in a long orange silk robe, an orange knit cap, and dark sunglasses, and he walked through the airport like a mini-prince passing through a congregation of devoted retainers.

"He likes toys," Rudi said to me when I asked him what kinds of gifts I should bring. "Especially orange ones that spin and bounce, like yo-yos, tops, and rubber balls. He likes orange socks, orange knit hats and orange sweaters, and he probably wears orange underwear."

The days blended into one another, meditation following meditation, *satsang* following *satsang*, Baba giving *shakti* and *prasad*, lecturing, chanting and welcoming hundreds of people, all crowding into the ashram. It was part circus, part carnival, part temple, and part spiritual mayhem, and all "The Baba Show". He told stories of great saints and *saddhus*, of gurus performing miracles in the jungles of India, of Nityananda who was beloved by tens of thousands of people. A small nucleus of devotees formed around Baba that somehow had a beeline into the inner circle of his life — a chosen few that he let near him, that cooked for him and served him. I looked on from the outer circle, never quite connecting to Baba, envious of those he let near him, and wondering why I couldn't get any closer.

Rudi had praised Baba to the sky. I kept looking up. I wanted to climb to the sky. Yet, I couldn't feel him in my heart. Though Baba had full billing and neon *shakti*, I saw only Rudi. Sometimes I felt alone and at odds with myself, wondering why I couldn't open to a great saint from the East; sometimes I felt like a young boy at the circus mesmerized by clowns.

My days were spent renovating a gallery in a building owned by Rudi that was next door to the meditation center. I scraped old wooden ceiling beams, and by ten in the morning, I looked like a coal miner, my face, arms, and hands covered with dirt and my clothes black. I spit dust and had a nose full of soot, and I'd peer out the gallery window at gaily–attired yogis gathered around Baba.

"The guru's God," Baba said. "Worship the guru. He's everything." "God is God," I heard Rudi say, "and at best the guru is his servant." "The guru is so pure that even a fly wouldn't land on him," Baba said. "I might not be so pure," Rudi said as a fly landed on his nose, "but at least I spend every minute of every day growing closer to God." "All you need is the guru's love," Baba said. "So chant his name. Sing *'Om Guru, Jai Guru, Nityananda Sada Guru.'* Chant his name and the guru will always be with you."

"I'd rather smoke dope than chant," Rudi said to me as we walked across the SMU campus in Dallas. "At least I'd know what was getting me stoned."

Smoke dope? I thought, laughing to myself. It's the only thing he forbids his students to do. Then I remembered him saying, "Never try to understand teachers. Just use their energy to get closer to God. Their purpose is to make disciples crazy. If you love your teacher more than God, then your teacher becomes your limitation. He's just a point in time and space, a step on a ladder into the cosmos. The guru–disciple relationship works because both surrender to God, not because they understand each other."

There was no understanding Baba. I didn't even try. From the moment he arrived, time suspended itself and seemed without beginning or end. The ashram was transformed into an enchanted castle of beaded, bearded, and robed *saddhus* from the West scurrying out of the New York City woodwork to meet a holy man from the East. Baba cast a spiritual spell on Rudi's students. Many of them turned on Rudi, declared Baba to be their teacher. I heard one of Rudi's ex–students say: "Rudi's a fat Jewish guy from Brooklyn. He eats meat and runs a business. How can I study with him?" A tug of war disrupted my inner quiet.

Then I heard Rudi say, "If Baba wants my students, my ashram, my business, my sex life, my teachings, they're all his. All I want in return is my spiritual enlightenment."

Baba demanded that Rudi stop teaching the open–eyed meditation that was the foundation of all his spiritual work. He demanded that Rudi become a vegetarian and celibate. So we chanted and sat in closed–eyed meditation, worshipped the guru, and picked out vegetarian dishes on menus in Chinatown.

"A cow doesn't eat meat, so why should we eat a cow?" Baba had said.

One morning, Rudi came into the gallery where I had been scraping beams. I stopped working and walked up to him. "It's Baba's way of taking over everything," he said. I could see that he was in pain. "But he can have it. My students don't belong to me; the ashram doesn't belong to me; nothing belongs to me. He's even gonna take Nityananda's soul out of me. I have to meet him in an hour. I want you to be there with me. I'll pass Nityananda's soul–force onto you and replace Nityananda with God. You remind me of him when he was a young *saddhu*. Sometimes I think it's the only reason I keep you as my student."

"Thank God for that," I said. He sat down on a chair and smiled.

"It's not so bad being celibate," he said. "If I can't have an orgasm, it doesn't mean I can't give someone else one. It doesn't mean I can't hold someone in my arms."

"I love you," I said. "You're my father and teacher and always will be."

"I promise, Stuart, I'll give you everything inside me," he said.

What more can I ask? I thought.

Days and nights of struggle are rewarded by the heart's goodness. A father begets a son who begets a son, each eternally begetting the other and transforming the other, and each passing down the teachings of God from generation to generation — each navigating a spiritual vessel through the ravages of time.

"I'm going to Dallas," Rudi said as he stood up. "Carr Collins invited Baba and myself and some other people. I'm going to ask him to include you in the group. You're my son, aren't you? Why shouldn't you go? He's in the store. Come and meet him."

"Like this?" I asked, looking at my filthy hands and clothing. Rudi shrugged and said, "What's the difference? Come on! If he can't see past some dirt, it's his problem."

My parents brought me into the world, I thought, and Rudi will guide me out...

What difference did it make if I was dressed in rags or in a tux, bow tie, and bowler hat? The magical child lived inside me. It lit my path, razed barriers, and equalized everything. It got me invited to all the right parties. When I sat with Rudi, I'd often feel like a child sitting in full lotus position in God's outstretched hand. The love he shared with me cleared a pathway to enlightenment.

Rudi and Baba struggled all the time. They were like two titans clashing on Tenth Street, Baba full of spiritual wisdom and Rudi trying to transform it into bite-sized pieces of food that were digestible.

"We've fed this turkey for a long time," Rudi said before Baba first arrived in America, "now we've got to eat him slice by slice."

"The halls of spiritual power are congested with saintly egos and wills," Rudi said as we continued our walk on the SMU campus, "and even jungle-bred *saddhus* fight for position like political power mongers. A taste of the American way overwhelms them. They begin to ask, 'Who is more holy? Who has more students? Who is God's chosen?' The answer is almost always, 'Me! I am!' It's a little frightening that holy men need to vie with each other for power."

But holy men are just men, I thought. They're human, and being human, they also have imperfections. It's not for me to judge them. I've got enough work to do to overcome my own limitations. When I think about it, their contradictions force me to go deeper inside myself. They force me to stop judging and to use their energy to get to God. To be right is to be dead. There's nowhere to go. Like Rudi once said—"Whatever works... Who gives a damn what costume it wears?"

"Om Guru, Jai Guru, Satchidananda Guru," we chanted while Baba sat center stage playing a tambourine, Rudi at his feet, with Baba's interpreter standing alongside and leading us in the mantra.

"Forget about the chanting and singing and all the histrionics," Rudi had said to me. "Just draw on Baba's energy. That's the secret of working with him. He's a great saint and a saint has to give *shakti* to disciples, *shakti* that'll help you get to God."

I sat on the floor, center-rear, keeping my eyes on Baba, breathing into my heart and below my navel. My eyes kept drifting to Rudi sitting on a pillow at Baba's feet, to Rudi, whose head spun and body shook, and who appeared to be in a trancelike state of otherworldly agony and bliss. The entire room turned black, then filled with golden light, and my astral body entered Rudi's heart. "The Guru is everything," Baba had said. I realized the truth of his words. "The Guru will give you life." Yes, Babaji, the Guru has given me life, I thought. He pulled me out of the gutter, trained me, and presented me to God. He put his and Nityananda's soul-force inside me. I discovered that my heart and Rudi's heart were the same, that love was the language of God and I had come to the earth to learn that language.

"God is love," Rudi had said many times in his lectures. "It's preached in every church, synagogue, and mosque. We hear it so much, we take it for granted; the same sermon preached week after week by minister after minister from the beginnings of time. Yet, if God is love, and Creation is love, and love is the soul of all living things, why is it so hard to find love in the world? Why is life's sweetness hidden beneath a boulder? Why is it that nothing makes sense?" Then he laughed for a moment, shrugged his shoulders, and said, "If the world made sense, it would be reduced to a boring, sterile reflection of the human mind. It would be a terrible place to live in."

There's no chance the world's gonna make sense, I thought. Sense or nonsense is nothing more or less than the fabric of living…

As for Baba, Nityananda, and all the itinerant *saddhus* in the jungles and mountains of India, as for all the *rinpoches* and *rishis* and anchorites and mendicant monks, I just didn't know. Their table must be set with a different kind of fare. It's hard to imagine Benares and New York City being on the earth at the same time. There must be many gods or one God in many forms, or maybe it's all the same thing; maybe religion is a matter of semantics. Certainly, Baba's way differs from Rudi's way, yet both are supposed to lead me to God.

It puzzled me why I couldn't find Baba in my heart. I searched for him there. Sometimes I got glimpses of him during deep meditation, but he would appear and disappear like some transient vision that refused to make itself at home.

"He's Rudi's teacher," I kept saying to myself. "Love him. Open to him. Receive his teachings."

Can the heart love transient visions? I asked myself. There's no consistency in them, nothing but air and spirit and color and form, nothing but an ongoing fairy tale pitting light and dark forces against each other. My heart aches because it's a human heart, needing to love and be loved, and to be grounded on the earth — a human heart, a place for loss and sorrow and gain.

"Om Guru, Jai Guru, Satchidananda Guru," I chanted silently to myself as we drove to the Big Indian ashram. It was Labor Day weekend. Crowds of people were expected to attend the convocation in honor of Baba. He would have *satsang* and give *prosad* and devotees from all over the United States would be able to pay homage to this great saint.

I've got to overcome my resistance to him, I thought. We had just passed the Newburgh exit and were heading north towards Kingston. I've got to make Baba my teacher the same way Rudi made Baba his teacher. Yet, when we arrived at the ashram, when the chanting started as well as the bowing and praying, I couldn't understand why my heart grew cold. I couldn't find Baba there. When I focused my attention on Rudi who sat at Baba's feet and worked nonstop to absorb *shakti*, I saw, for the first time in my life, the power of surrender. Rudi revealed to me the guts it took to have a spiritual life.

The weekend's festivities continued nonstop. We welcomed Eastern religion like beggars welcoming a Thanksgiving meal. The Aquarian Age had begun. We sang and danced and prayed and loved, and swirls and twirls of burning incense rose from our ashram to heaven. An adult never grows old if he stays a kid in his heart; a kid never turns his back on life's possibilities; a kid is a prophet of love in a time of hate and anger and joy and bliss; flower children join hands and dance in a circle of innocence. No more promises, I thought. No more platitudes and sitcoms and mundane preachers of gospel. Just this circle, this dance — in many ways it was like Genesis.

I listened to Baba's ageless wisdom rooted in Vedic stories, in the *Bhagavad Gita*, in the *Ramayana*, in the holy mystique of Indian lore, and I tasted a spiritual nectar at the tip of my tongue that flowed from the crown of my head like a brook trickling down the side of a mountain; and I thought the ashram was a holy place, and Rudi was a holy being, and Baba was a saintly man, and, perhaps for the first time in my life, there was nothing wrong with the world.

Then Baba said: "Nityananda lives in the Blue World — a world of transcendental bliss. If you meditate on the Blue World, you will be free. So take the Blue World into your heart and mind and let the light of the Blue World fill your being. It will heal you. It will guide you. It will give you a glimpse of eternity."

It gave me a glimpse of a ten–foot spider projected on the screen of my mind with legs dangling and tentacles floating in and out of the Blue World. My head ached and my legs ached and the walls about me crumbled. I was seated, full lotus, on top a blue ridge that capped the highest mountain on earth — a jumping jack in a flack jacket, warding off pellets of time and space. I experienced every kind of hallucination but a Blue World.

Baba got up and left the room. He returned to his quarters, and Rudi taught a mediation class. The light in the blue room turned gold and halo–like radiances shot out of Rudi's head and heart. Tears covered my face and I was lifted up to a place where Rudi and I walked hand in hand before God. I kissed Rudi's foot and bowed reverently before the infinite.

After the class, Rudi hugged each of his students and his sweet *shakti* threaded heart–to–heart, finger–to–finger, and his sweet *shakti* opened my *chakra* system and sent me flying across the Big Indian lawn. I saw stars and lights and gods and goddesses. I didn't know if I was asleep or awake, but I couldn't stand up. Five minutes or ten minutes or ten days or five years later, Nityananda descended from the Blue World and entered my heart. He lay down next to me and I slept with him in my arms. In a dream, Rudi touched my forehead with his finger. My body twisted and turned and jerked, and my spine arched like a rainbow. One moment I witnessed myself turn into a ninety year–old man, and, in the next I was a fetus; at one moment pairs of skeletons danced near me, in the next I was playing volleyball with childhood chums. I saw myself chanting sutras in an ancient Tibetan monastery, and I saw the earth tilting on its axis, as thousands of converging rivers poured their water into eternity. Five minutes or ten minutes or ten years later, I got up and looked for Rudi. He was holding a sixty year–old Indian man in his arms as if the man were his own child. The Indian man was crying — his grey head resting on Rudi's chest, his arms held Rudi like a loving son. Many people were sitting at Rudi's feet. They chanted *"Sri Ram, Jai Ram, Jai Ram, Ram Om,"* and others walked hand in hand across the lawn, and others tossed a Frisbee, and others played flutes and drums and guitars, and others sat in meditation, and others watched in disbelief as Rudi performed psychic surgery on his students, and all of us basked in the unconditional love pouring out of Rudi's heart — a love given freely to whomever wanted it.

I dilly–dallied in Baba's Blue World, but wasn't sure if there was any difference between worlds that were blue or yellow or red or green. Perhaps the Blue World was a refuge for *saddhus* that had already taken *samadhi*, I thought. Baba's presence had definitely changed something in me. If nothing else, it forced me to get rid of whatever preconceptions, opinions and spiritual ideas I had. I didn't know at the time whether it was Baba's presence that accomplished these minor miracles or the way Rudi used everything he got from Baba, both positive and negative, to get closer to his own God–realization. The significance of guru became important to me, but even more important than that was a simple thing that I learned from Baba. He made it clear to me that Rudi was my root guru.

Rudi and Baba, and myself, as well as an orange–clad entourage of men and women, flew to Dallas as guests of Carr Collins and his wife. We stayed at the Hilton Inn. We followed Baba around like a flock of spiritual chicks in a coop. He gave talks at yoga centers, churches, and he held *darshan* in his hotel quarters. His magnetic presence seduced people into serving him. Crowds of people gathered in Baba's presence, and many among them were professionals, housewives, and bedraggled hippies looking stoned and starving for some kind of meditation practice. During a visit to the World of Animals, Rudi pointed to a lion and told Baba that lion steak is on the menu tonight. "Lions eat meat, don't they? So we can eat lions."

Baba laughed at Rudi's mirthful irreverence and then placed his finger on Rudi's forehead. Rudi's neck swirled and his spine arched and his eyes rolled back into his head. He entered a deep trance. Baba sat quietly in the front seat of the car. He seemed to enjoy the parade of passing animals. When Rudi came out of his trance, he kissed Baba's hand, and thanked him.

"There are a group of young people that invited me to their home in Denton," Rudi said to Baba, referring to the longhaired hippie–types that came to Baba's talks. "I think they're ripe for an ashram. Should I go?"

Baba nodded yes. The next day, Rudi and I drove to Denton, Texas. "I think ashrams are going to spring up everywhere," Rudi said. "I'm beginning to see my work for the next ten years."

Rudi and I spent eighteen hours a day together and he spoke incessantly about his spiritual life and relationship with Baba. What he imparted was street wisdom in machine–gun fashion. He transformed ancient Hindu texts into something I could understand. Somehow, he and Baba grew distant from each other. I didn't know if it was caused by an ego clash, cultural differences, differences in teaching methods, or what, but I sensed a rift, and I sensed that Rudi's real work was just beginning. Nothing was said. The days passed in silent acceptance of the problem. Baba's closest disciples snubbed us. I didn't care. It meant that I had no competition for Rudi's time. It meant that I could spend eighteen hours every day we were in Dallas, learning from my spiritual master.

"It's like trying to figure out why dragons fight in the cosmos," Rudi laughed. "I don't understand the impossible. I can only surrender to it and transform it into Higher Consciousness. All I want is my God–realization; all I want is to be free."

Late one afternoon, while Rudi napped in his hotel room, I sat at the foot of his bed in deep meditation and witnessed a strange transformation take place. One moment he was Rudi, the next, Baba, and the next, Swami Nityananda. When he awoke, he asked me what I saw. I told him. He smiled, sat up on the bed and hugged me. "I'm really changing," he said. "I'm getting ready to absorb all of Baba's teachings and go on." I looked at my watch.

"It's time for Baba's *darshan*," I said.

A small group of disciples gathered in Baba's quarters every day in the late afternoon and meditated with him for about half an hour. Sometimes he'd talk about the ancient texts and about applying the guru's grace to living in the world. Every day, about three-quarters of the way through *darshan*, he'd ask me when I would visit him at his ashram in Ganeshpuri, India. "I don't know," I repeated time and again until I began feeling silly. One afternoon, before *darshan*, I retired to my hotel room and meditated. I needed an answer for Baba. I felt like a fool going "gaga" before a great spiritual master. I reached deeper and deeper into my unconscious self, until the astral body of Swami Nityananda came out of my heart and sat on the bed in front of me.

"You'll go to Ganeshpuri when Rudi sends you there," Swami Nityananda said.

"Thank you, my grandfather," I answered him.

Of course, that's the answer, I thought. Baba teaches that the guru is everything. Rudi gave me my life. He's my guru. If I love him, respect him, and learn from him, his teachings will take me all the way to God.

At *darshan*, Baba asked me once again when I would be coming to visit him in Ganeshpuri. "When Rudi sends me," I said grateful to have an answer to his question.

After *darshan*, while in the hotel corridor waiting for Rudi, one of Baba's disciples asked me to follow him. "Baba wants to speak with you. He's in his quarters." I followed him, unsure of what Baba wanted with me, but happy to be summoned for a private consultation.

"You love Rudi," Baba said.

"Yes," I answered.

"He's your guru."

"Yes."

Baba opened a clothes closet, reached in, and took a long orange silk robe off a hanger. He gave it to me. "Wear it when you meditate," he said. "You will be a great teacher someday." I thanked him with tears in my eyes, then kissed his hands and feet, and left his quarters. I looked for Rudi. I wanted to show him the robe and to share with him what Baba said to me. I wanted to thank Rudi for teaching me the true nature of guru...

I open my eyes. The fog has grown thicker. It blocks my vision and makes me fearful that we've lost our way. "I'm leaving for Europe this weekend to begin a deeper commitment towards my European ashrams," Rudi dictates to Mimi. "Most of the teachers in the United States were brought to New York for additional work and a strengthening of existing connections between us..."

"In a few minutes, we'll be low enough to see the ground," Beau whispers to me.

I don't know if the ground is up or down or beside me or located somewhere at earth's end, I think. I take Rudi's hand. We're nestled in time's embrace. The black-grey fog forms skeleton-like images with large socket-less eyes and open mouths spitting black fire. "Do you have a piece of fruit?" I ask Mimi. Are we going up or down, I ask myself? She shrugs her shoulders and says, "No." I hope there are no mountains above the Hudson. I hope we land soon...

I close my eyes again.

"I want you to spend a week in Denton," Rudi said to me at the Hilton Inn hotel in Dallas, "teaching our meditation to those young people." He and Baba, and the others were going to San Antonio and then Los Angeles.

I'm three weeks ahead of those kids, I thought, and now I'm to going to play spiritual teacher; I don't know who I am or what I am; I don't know if I'm a true vehicle for God or a fool in an orange t-shirt talking a good rap. Rudi believes in me. I wish I could believe in myself. I wish I could secure my connection with Higher Energy. Those kids are young and anxious to learn, and so am I.

"Teaching is learning," Rudi said before he left for San Antonio. "Every one of those kids will show you your limitations."

I drove thirty miles north of Dallas to Denton — a small university town in North Texas. I drove through flat, endless stretches of land on either side of a highway lined with billboards, motels, and fast food outlets, land covered by a vast sky — a no man's land seemingly one step from the end of the earth. I expected John Wayne to ride out of a pasture. I expected the sky to fall and the grass to roll up.

My first task in Denton was to get the "flower children" to flush their drugs down the toilet. I told them it's the only taboo in the ashram. So thousands of dollars worth of grass, LSD, and whatever, vanished into the sewer system beneath Denton. Agonizing flush after agonizing flush rid them of their dope. We began meditation classes, and a bond grew between us. They loved Rudi, and respected me as his disciple. When the week ended, I was sorry to leave. I told them we'd see each other again.

After Baba left for India and Rudi returned to New York, the teachings at the ashram underwent a drastic change. We no longer practiced open–eyed meditation, but chanted, prayed, meditated with our eyes closed, and transformed a once–familiar environment into a Hindu–type school resembling ashrams in India. Baba wanted us to live in the guru's grace. He said that was all we needed.

Dogma crept into my life — vegetarianism, celibacy, and devotional yoga. A bevy of new students sought spiritual solace from Rudi. He shared with us the fruits of his work with Baba. "I've been cut to pieces," he said, "and now I've got to put myself back together."

Many of his old students left. They rejected Rudi and chose Baba as their root guru. But many more came vying for Rudi's time and attention. The number of people in the ashram doubled or tripled and Rudi projected that thousands more would come. "How are you going to teach a thousand people?" one disciple asked. "I'll take them into my heart," Rudi answered, "love them and find room for them inside me. It's just another opportunity to grow." My private sessions with Rudi were a thing of the past. I had to work differently with him; I had to share him with many others.

"The *siddha* domain is in the Blue World," Rudi said to me one afternoon in his store, "but I don't want to be trapped in any world. I want a direct connection with infinite energy in the Universe. I don't believe God is limited to one vision of the cosmos. I mean, people experience the astral plane and make a big deal about it, but the astral plane is more like a cosmic slum where science–fiction–type creatures beckon us with open arms. I don't want to hang out there. I'd rather be a speck of light dissolving into the eternal. It strikes me that, after awhile, even heaven itself can become a bore. How long can we sit around looking at and praising the Pearly Gates without boredom setting in? I don't think I would want to decorate my apartment in pastels. There's no way we can define Higher Consciousness. It's an energy that transcends logic, understanding, and rational thinking. We can only experience it through surrender.

"Enlightenment is a lifetime's work," he went on. "Most people think three percent of consciousness is something terrific. They grope through life like sheep lost in a fog..."

Like our Cessna airplane, I chuckle nervously to myself. Beau's fingers are fidgeting with the instruments and there's a worried look on his face.

"It takes so long to find God," Rudi once said in his store.

Where's he hiding? I think. Can he be watching us from behind the black clouds engulfing our plane?

"A lot of people are staying in your house," I said to Rudi while Baba was in New York. "Do you think after he leaves that I can live there too? I'd like to be close to you. I want to learn everything you have to teach."

He looked at me with an appraising twinkle in his eye. Then he addressed another student who sat next to him. "Stuart wants to live in the ashram. Should we let him? He thinks that it will give him a spiritual life." When he turned to me, there was a big smile on his face. "Of course," he said. "You're one of my sons, aren't you? I need you to be close to me." I hugged and thanked him. "We've got important work to do, Stuart. You've got to get your training."

The changes in Rudi were apparent. He asked me if I could see what was happening in his forehead and pointed his finger to a place just above the eyebrows that I knew was the location of the third eye. "A psychic channel connects the center of my forehead to the top of my head and spiritual energy flows from one to the other," he said. I could clearly see what he was talking about. The lines in his head resembled the wings of a phoenix bird and a clear indentation marked the third eye. "At all times, I hear the OM sound. It enters my system through the crown *chakra* and helps strengthen each of the seven energy centers inside me." He placed his finger on my forehead and the room suddenly filled with light. My back arched, and my inner life soared through a void-like emptiness to a space with soft golden colors. A high-pitched, electronic sound pierced my crown *chakra* and vibrated inside me. "I need strong and devoted students," Rudi said when I came out of my trance. "I need to find my four sons." He shrugged his shoulders and said: "Very few people understand life; very few people are willing to pay the price."

But it costs so little, I thought, if I compare a spiritual life with other possibilities.

His house was a mini–paradise full of ancient Oriental sculptures, paintings, rugs, Buddhas and Bodhisattvas, gods, goddesses, and cosmic creatures from every Eastern culture. I'd roll out my sheepskin bedding beneath a six–foot–high bronze statue of *L'Amo*, the goddess who protected the country of Tibet. She rode on a donkey with two lion–headed *dakinis* at her side, valiantly warding off evil spirits, and did a great job of protecting me from myself.

But two months of exotic living came to an abrupt halt when twelve yogis from Texas arrived at Rudi's house, twelve young men and women, all of them bright–eyed and full of love. They parked themselves alongside me on the second floor — sleeping bags, backpacks and all — transforming paradise into a dormitory. Day followed frenzied day until two weeks of close–quarter living nearly drove me insane. I didn't have a place to sleep. I'd stand in line every morning to pee. Two weeks became twelve months as the Texas yogis were followed by hundreds of disciples from all over the world. There were never less than six people living on the second floor at any one time, and sometimes as many as twenty. I tripped over sleeping bodies in the dark, cleaned toilets, sinks, vacuumed floors, and cooked breakfast for twenty–some–odd people every morning; and to add insult to injury, I had to account to Rudi if things went wrong. I cursed discipleship. My spiritual romance with Rudi came to an end and months of inner turmoil followed.

"To live is to struggle," Rudi once said to a group of students in his store. "The alternative is to die, and then all pain disappears, all sorrow and disappointment disappear. Most people desperately want to graze in their own personal pasture and not be hassled by anything. A goat eats and sleeps, pays no rent, and supports nothing. But human beings struggle. They have desires and ambitions and fears. They want to love and be loved, and to build lives for themselves. At the same time, they covet the two–hour day. They complain about life's responsibilities and would rather stare at television sets or spend time doing nothing than take full responsibility for themselves. We suffer anyway, whether we want to or not. So we might as well pay for our lives consciously; we might as well use our energies to attain spiritual enlightenment."

Rudi and I paid a visit to the home of two of his friends. One of our hosts asked Rudi why people live in his house the way they do.

"No one likes living in the ashram," he answered laughing and nudging me. "Right, Stuart?" I smiled and said, "Yes." "They're in my house to learn to have a spiritual life. If they don't get training, they'll never be able to teach my work. It's easy to keep your heart open when everything's going well, but the real test is to keep your heart open while taking out the garbage. Most of life is about taking out the garbage, anyway, and most people are unhappy. I bet you think ashrams are holy places inhabited by angelic people. But bliss, radiance, and love are states of grace that manifest after years of inner work. Most sweetness in people is a veneer that peels up in harsh weather. It has no depth or permanence. It disappears when they suffer."

The second floor housed a flock of Western *nagababas* come home to their spiritual father to roost. Not a night passed when I didn't think about running away. I could always go to Ganeshpuri and see Baba, I'd think, or just do an about-face and return to my solitary lifestyle. Rudi's days and nights were given to expanding the ashram. There were always at least fifteen people for breakfast and twenty people for dinner. The second floor of his house was like a mini Grand Central Station. People came and left all the time. They were all students and were attracted to Rudi because of the nature of his teachings. Every evening, before and after dinner, he would sit in half-lotus position on his chair and dispense *shakti* to every person living in his house. He never charged money for classes. He told me that his teachers didn't charge. Gratitude for his life made him work as hard as he did to uplift other people. If it weren't for Nityananda and the Shankaracharya, he probably would be dead today.

The meditations were so profound that you could see students changing in front of your eyes. Many of them competed for his attention. Though I never thought myself a jealous person, I lived day after day with jealousy staring me in the face. It sniped at me from the unconscious. I had to struggle against an enemy I never knew existed, an enemy that stood between my spiritual life and me.

"Human beings can change," Rudi would say when he spoke after meditation class. "They have choice, and choice separates them from animals. On the other side of each and every one of us is God, and we create all the blocks, barriers, and obstacles that separate us from spiritual enlightenment. I've heard teachers say that the mind is the slayer of the soul. But if we use the mind as energy, if we focus the mind's energy on the *chakra* below the navel, if we use it as a surgical instrument, and open the center of foundation and balance in us, what is killing us can give us life. The objective world is more of a dream than the dreams we have when asleep; it is a mere reflection of the truth and it changes as the inner life of a human being changes. We've got to use everything to get closer to God."

"I've got no place to sleep," I said to Rudi, eight months into my stay at his house." Did you come to the ashram to sleep," he asked me, "or to learn about God? It takes guts to grow; it takes guts to give up everything to learn from your teacher and to be grateful for it. Only survivors become enlightened," and he pointed to a weed growing in a crack in the sidewalk. "That weed has more life in it than you," he said as he walked into his store and greeted a client.

I wanted to beat my fists against a brick building. I wanted to run away. But where would I go? I thought. To my past...to a Spanish jail...to cold October nights sleeping by the Seine? And I stopped and thought for a minute...to God? Then there's no escaping the second floor of his house! There's no escaping the guru and his teachings.

The great green weed grew in my mind's eye until it rose above the buildings and wrapped itself around the sun. I climbed it like Jack climbing the beanstalk. I climbed and climbed until the heat of the sun dried up my thoughts, until I breathed fresh air, and quieted my mind. "Even if?" I said to myself. "But there are no "even ifs" anymore.

There are only weeds struggling for life in New York City sidewalk cracks, I think. I look out the window at a persistent fog swallowing up our plane, close my eyes and once again listen to my thoughts.

"You need to go back to school," Rudi said to me one day in his store. "You need to get a degree in education. If I send you to Big Indian to teach, you've got to have a way of supporting yourself."

"College?" I smiled.

"Yeah," he answered. "What's so funny?"

"I hate college."

"Then learn to like it," he said. "It's about time you learned to finish cycles, to bring something in your life to an end. Anyway, when you graduate, wonderful things are going to happen to you."

What does college have to do with a spiritual life, I thought as I entered the meditation room. I'd rather roast *chappatis* on a Ganges *ghat*. I've no need to discuss world problems or analyze the socio-economic plight of third-world countries or plunge into the profundity of Aristotle or Plato. None of these subjects relate to street life in New York

City; none of these subjects relate to *chakras*, inner work, and getting to God. But, Rudi's right about my never finishing anything. All my life, I've run away from both success and failure. If I go back to school, if I get a degree, if I listen to Rudi, I can demand more from him, I can take his teachings deeper.

I registered for a humanities degree at The New School for Social Research, took classes in the morning, worked in the afternoon, taught *hatha* yoga at five in the evening, meditated with Rudi, and studied far into the night. My resistance to school broke down when I recognized that I was not there to learn philosophy, literature and psychology, but to learn patience, and how to stop fighting with and judging my teachers. They're just human beings, I thought, and they struggle with their own lives. It didn't matter if I was right or they were right, or if they bored me or I bored them, what mattered was that we saw the humanity in each other. Going to college forced me to reappraise my life on the second floor. I had turned paradise into hell. Rudi was my main connection to God — my umbilical cord at this moment. My fellow yogis on the second floor were there for the same reason. "Love them," I repeated over and over to myself. "Have patience with them, because if I can't forgive them their minor indiscretions, who the hell is ever going to forgive me."

"You can relax, Stuart," Rudi said to me one day in his store. "I'm sending everyone home." I smiled and said to him, "It doesn't matter. You can invite a hundred more students if you want. They've all served me. I'm grateful to them. They've helped me to get free of myself."

"That's why I invited them here in the first place. You had to get this training. Without it, you'd never fulfill your life's work."

"A little lower," Beau whispers. "Just a little lower and I'll see the ground."

I turn to Rudi and try to do my meditation exercise. So often words say less than a smile or the squeeze of a hand. I was a spiritually gifted kid once who fought with my guru, only to learn that my guru's love was without limitation.

"We're at 6200 feet," Beau whispers.

No sign of the Hudson, I think, while I look out the window. No sign of trees, houses, headlights or street lamps...

"I do not wish to exchange my loyalties in this country for those in another," Rudi dictates. "It's easy to look to the glamour of a foreign culture as a means of expansion. But the success of our work will be based on the depth and growth and love that exists between me and those to whom I've committed my life. From that integrity the European

ashrams can grow."

"It's not easy to discover that tension is a healthy thing and essential for inner growth," Rudi once said to me in his store. "It's not easy to discover that resistance is the key to change and rebirth. The real work is building the *chakra* system and transforming our tension into a life–giving force. When we've learned to sustain happiness, we've learned everything that we have to learn on earth. We're finished with our karma. It's all so simple that it slips past most people who want satisfaction, power and success, and are focused solely on material attainment."

How many times have I been slain by Rudi's invisible sword that would cut away large chunks of my ego. I'd sit on the banks of the Rudi River and watch my garbage float downstream. Then he'd offer me a bagel, lox, and cream cheese sandwich, hug me, and talk about us moving to the Middle East, about us finding the teacher of the Aquarian Age — a six year–old kid who, at this moment, might be living in a brothel in Cairo.

Mostly, I had to learn to survive...

Living on the second floor helped me to get closer to Rudi. A spiritual bond grew between us, one that transcended interpersonal relationships, a closeness based on two people's need to be enlightened. I found a father, brother, and friend, but, above all, I found the one person who could reveal to me the ways of God in the world.

When will the fog lift? I think. When will I see the Hudson River again? When will I see millions of twinkling stars in the sky: the Milky Way, Ursa Minor and Major, the Big and Little Dipper, the entire mythological playground of twinkling balls of light; when the fog lifts and clear vision rids the threat of danger...how similar this flight is to my own life, to my spiritual journey. I once saw a painting of a staff in Rudi's store by a Japanese Zen master who wrote in sprawling calligraphy on one side of the staff, 'those who are on the path get hit by this stick,' and on the other side 'those who are not on the path get hit by this stick.' A Japanese friend of mine translated it for me. I laughed and said to myself that a wise man suffers with an open heart and uses his suffering to get to God.

"What about food?" I asked Rudi at the Second Avenue Deli. Meditation class was in fifteen minutes, and he wanted to get a quick hot dog.

"You can eat shit," he answered, "and if you're pure inside, it'll turn to gold."

Like St. Francis in Kazantzakis's novel, I thought, eating dirt and dust and roots and shrubs, and scorning rich people who complained about his life and diet.

"Many food fanatics substitute diet for a spiritual life," Rudi went on. "They're so engrossed in what they eat that they forget it's just a diet and that diet doesn't elevate their consciousness to a superior position on the planet. They preach the benefits of a certain diet, and forget that what works for one person doesn't necessarily work for another. I mean, Tibetans eat meat and Indians eat vegetables. It doesn't make Indians more spiritual than Tibetans. Imagine living fifteen thousand feet above sea level in a barren, mountainous, snow–covered landscape and surviving on a diet of lentils and brown rice. It's almost laughable. Some of us need to be vegetarians, others meat–eaters, others macrobiotics, others fruitarians; but each person needs to determine this for himself. It's very difficult to find what works for oneself, but even more difficult to practice it without trying to convert everyone you meet."

I had spent many hours in macrobiotic restaurants eating brown rice, sauteed vegetables, pinto beans and tofu, and listening to people talk ad nauseam about brown rice: how long to boil it, soak it, chew it. Is it organically grown? What brands are the best? Should you eat long grain or short grain...and on and on until I had visions of my macrobiotic soul mates being reincarnated as grains of brown rice. The conversations drove me to distraction. I started eating at home and went to jazz clubs with a friend. I'd sip some soda water, listen to the music, and talk about anything but brown rice.

"There's nothing worse than being right all the time," Rudi said as we walked back from the Second Avenue Deli to his meditation center. "Have you ever spent time with people that are never wrong? They're like mummies walking slowly to the grave. They've nowhere else to go! I'd rather be wrong all the time. At least I can learn something, at least I'm not judging everyone and everything according to my preconceptions, and at least there's room for humility and growth."

I close my eyes and try to relax. Another half–hour and we'll be in Glens Falls. Just another half hour — the propeller's whir is a backdrop to Rudi's voice: "The investment of people who have been with me that allows our work to consciously deepen and expand." Can my dark premonitions be averted? Can my fear be quelled? I remember Rudi saying that fear is natural and healthy. It's a reminder to us that we're human, that danger does exist in the world. "The real problem is the mind," he said in one of his talks. "Once it gets involved, minor sensations of fear get out of control. They become larger–than–life–size demons that live inside us. The secret is to starve fear and not to let it feed the mind and cripple us. The worst thing that can happen is we die. Then there's nothing else to worry about. No more fear, unhappiness, and anxiety. The struggle is over. We can take a rest."

I listen to my breathing, and Rudi takes my hand. He squeezes it, and suddenly the fear is removed from my body. His soft, moist hand holds mine, and each of his fingers pulsates with energy. "It's not the neurotic need to go off to foreign lands," he dictates, his five burning fingers cutting through my palm as if lasers were sending jolts of energy to my heart, throat and navel *chakra*s.

"Hello! Hello!" Beau whispers. The radio is in his hand.

The worst thing that can happen is getting lost in life and not finding your way out, I think. Death is a reprieve from our private and public hells...

"Hello!"

No answer.

"It's not death that's the problem, but the fear of life," Rudi said to me as we were walking on Fourth Avenue. "I spent too many youthful days searching for a true picture of myself, only to discover that the self doesn't exist. It's nothing more than thousands of fragmented images of me vying with each other for recognition. I stopped looking for self and decided instead to build an inner life that would connect me with God. If I transformed all those images of self into nothing, there would be a place for Higher Creative Energy to come and live inside me. I could get my enlightenment."

Six years with Rudi, I think, seem like a thousand quick years that have touched on Eternity.

"I'd rather surrender to God," Rudi said. We had just entered his store, and he waved to his mother, "than carry around a suitcase full of knowledge about myself."

Me too, I think, and I understand much less than he does.

I could feel his hand in mine and I could sense Beau nervously trying to guide our plane.

It was nine o'clock Sunday night, and we had just returned to Rudi's house from Big Indian. The telephone rang. It was one of Rudi's students who told him that he had left his camera in the car. Rudi asked me to get it. On the way back from the garage to his house, a group of teenage boys jumped me and stole the camera. "What happened?" Rudi asked when he saw me. I must've been white as a sheet.

"I was mugged," I answered. "At the corner of Tenth Street and Fourth Avenue."

He sat down on the couch, crossed his legs beneath him, and motioned for me to sit at his feet. He breathed deeply into his heart and navel *chakra,* and took my wrist in his hand. We both entered a deep state of meditation. In a matter of seconds, my hand disappeared in a golden aura of light. It was replaced by Nityananda's hand. Then all I saw was a translucent hand — an ethereal, otherworldly manifestation of pure golden color where once I saw my own hand.

"You'll be able to heal people in the future," Rudi said after the meditation ended. "I also put a protective force around you — a pair of spiritual bodyguards. They'll watch out for you."

I sat in disbelief and thought that it was more science fiction than reality. At first, I treated my cosmic guardians with tongue–in–cheek, calling them Heckle and Jeckle and kidding them whenever my life got difficult. But, in time, I realized what Rudi had given me; I realized the blessed nature of protective divinities and the sacredness of Nityananda's hand. The world is a crazy place and it could be quite dangerous, I thought. Now I can walk through it without fear. Nobody will believe me if I tell them, but, who cares? The ways of Rudi are sacred and best kept quiet; the ways of God will always be a mystery to me.

From that moment on, in every meditation class, I'd see Rudi and Nityananda sitting in my palm of my right hand, and a golden aura of light surrounded them. Sometimes, I'd even see a blue *mandala* of whirling energy emanate from my heart. As the months passed, I noticed that the wings of a Phoenix bird appeared in my forehead. My heart and mind became less bothered by the cares of ordinary life and I finally accepted the constant companionship of my cosmic bodyguards.

It was a hot July morning at the Big Indian ashram and I walked with Rudi through the vegetable garden. Meditation class would be in an hour. He kneeled and picked a few ripe tomatoes. "For my mother," he smiled. "You can't get them like this in the supermarkets." We continued to walk and he asked me if I was ready to go to the Middle East. "My bags are packed," I joked. "We'll go there and buy fifty acres of beachfront property and build an ashram that'll attract the teacher of the Aquarian Age. He'll be my student. I'll train him in our work, and he'll guide thousands of people through the *Kali Yuga*." He stopped talking for a short while, and then, from a sad, almost introverted place, he continued: "He'll be a kid, and he'll get crucified and be a sacrificial lamb for a New Age. I often think it's better to be the teacher of Christ than Christ Himself. Who wants all the press, anyway?"

After the noonday meditation class and before lunch, I sat alone near the apple orchard. I thought about Rudi's four sons — who they'd be, where they'd teach; and I thought about the teacher of the Aquarian Age living in a brothel in the Middle East, and I thought that no place on earth is more sacred than any other. The earth is always in transition. Mountain ranges become prairies, and deserts mountain ranges. Nature understands this and people need to sit at Nature's feet and learn something important.

The sky over Big Indian was clear, and the summer air was filled with the songs of blue jays and robins. The distant sound of a brook meshed with voices of people lounging on the ashram lawn, and I could feel the sun heating my body. There was a feeling in me that time had stopped. God was in the world, and Big Indian the perfect place to be.

"There's a full moon tonight," Rudi said in the dining hall, "and we're going to have a fire *puja*. Get some shovels and picks, and we'll dig a ditch on the hill above the garden."

"What's a *puja*?" one of his students asked.

"It's a purification rite by fire," he replied, "a time to burn something you possess as an offering to the gods."

As Rudi and I walked to the site, he said to me, "My head's coming apart. It feels like cosmic physicians are cutting away bone and marrow, making room for a new level of spiritual work. The pain exceeds anything I've felt before. I've just got to survive. I've got to have patience."

He heard me talk about my poetry to one of his students. I had brought the sole manuscript of my writings with me to show to a friend and Rudi suggested that we use it to start the *puja* fire. I looked at him with horror on my face. He picked up a stone and threw it into the pit. He's got to be joking, I thought. But his words struck home. They made me realize how attached I was to my poems, and I remembered him saying that detachment was the first step to spiritual enlightenment.

At 9:00 PM Rudi tried to start the fire, but couldn't get the logs to burn. Nothing worked. He looked at me disgustedly and said, "I need your manuscript." I went and got it. He lit the pages, and, like magic, the twigs caught fire, the logs caught fire, and the *puja* began.

I watched my life go up in smoke, but instead of feeling sorrow, I laughed and cried and danced and chanted, and I ripped off my shirt and threw it into the fire. I entered a trancelike state and was determined to make a new beginning. I was determined to never tie another albatross around my neck.

Once again, I look out of the plane's window, and the black cloud-like soup seems darker than before.

"Headed north," Beau whispers into the radio. "Lowering my altitude. Can you read me?"

"Beau!" I whisper to him.

"Not now! I'm busy!"

Maybe we should go back, I think. But I have no idea where back or forward is. I turn to Rudi.

"Beau," Mimi says in a soft voice.

"Not now! I'm busy!" I hear him say again.

The problem in life is that every one's too busy, I think angrily. Being busy is like being religious. It justifies our lives. It predisposes arrogance. We can talk down to other people. We can be more important than them.

I breathe into my navel *chakra* and the anger subsides, and for a moment, I forget about Beau and the fog and I turn to Rudi.

"A woman's at her most beautiful when she's pregnant," he said to his mother and myself one day in the store. "There's the seed of life in her, and she's focused day and night on the navel *chakra* — the very foundation of her being. The miracle of birth is that a new soul arrives on earth and has the potential to attain spiritual enlightenment. A pregnant woman is the vehicle for that soul, and she is the servant of a universe striving for perfection."

He stopping talking for a moment and took a sip of coffee. Then he looked lovingly at his mother and said, "It takes nine months to have a baby and one second to die, and those nine months of pregnancy teach every woman patience, forgiveness, unconditional love, and surrender — all qualities that fill her with divine beauty. I feel, Mama, as if I've been pregnant for twenty years," he laughed, "as if I carry a spiritual child in my belly and my goal is to stay pregnant for the rest of my life."

But where are we going now, Rudi dear? I think. The plane is at four thousand feet and we're flying through a fog to a small town near Albany. I've never been to Albany or Glens Falls, and I'd probably never go there if it weren't for you. It seems like the longer we fly, the thicker the "soup" becomes.

They tell me that there was a time when people treated each other with respect, a time when water was purer, food fresher, when people didn't die from cancer, when it was safe to walk the streets. They tell me that today's not what it used to be. It seems as though the "days of innocence" have been lost in clouds of mounting pressure, anxiety, and resentment; it seems as if those days exist mostly in memory and in a longing to recapture the past. Sometimes I think our lives border on "days of innocence," and I think we've no recourse but to deal with each day as it comes, and survival depends upon us opening our hearts and embracing our inner child.

"A spiritual life isn't a part–time job," Rudi once said to me in his store. It was a late winter's afternoon, overcast and looking as if it were getting ready to snow. "It's not something you do once a month or when you're in the mood. It requires daily work, effort and consciousness. Most people's practice of meditation is more an adult education course than spiritual work. They fit it in when they have time...once a week, twice a month...whenever the business of life permits a spare moment. There's always an excuse for not doing it. I have a party, a date, a business meeting, I've scratched myself...I've got a headache...whatever. Most people's immediate concerns go no further than money, what's between their legs, relationships, power and inadequacy; most people — at forty years of age — are emotionally seven and intellectually nine, yet we expect them to act like adults. But they never live up to our expectations. They find it impossible to live in the moment. Their lack of forgiveness stunts emotional and intellectual growth.

"If I can't love myself, it's impossible to love anyone else," Rudi went on. "It all starts there. Then I can extend that love to my mother and my students and to anyone who comes into my life. I can look past their limitations. I can nurture the seed of life in them. Someone once asked me why gurus wear orange all the time. 'It's the color of surrender,' I said. 'But what are you surrendering?' I thought for a moment and answered: 'Tension. You see, orange is the color of fire. Fire rises and falls, changes its form, but above all else, it transforms everything into ashes and smoke.'"

"Can we turn back?" I whisper to Beau. He's still busy with the instruments.

"I'm not sure which way that is," he says.

The altimeter shows 3800 feet, but I can't see the ground. That's higher than the Empire State Building, I think, than the Chrysler Building or a radio tower. I'm not sure if I'm supposed to be scared.

"A little lower," Beau says. "A little lower and we'll see the ground. There was nothing like this in the weather report. It's got to clear up soon."

It was late one night in Big Indian. I was standing on a hill and looking at a clear vast expanse of sky, a sky unencumbered by city lights that reminded me of a pure heart in a motionless ocean of energy in which I could lose myself. I remember thinking how quiet it was, how I couldn't hear a bird or a frog or a cricket, and I remember thinking if only my mind would shut up...

"I need to strengthen and clarify my relationships with all my close teachers before I leave," Rudi dictated to Mimi.

The relationship I have with myself keeps shifting and changing, I think. It seems like the only clear relationship I have in my life is with Rudi. I look at him again and smile. I remember a time at Big Indian on a late summer's morning I was digging a ditch in the ashram's front yard. My arms were aching and body sweating, and my shoes, trousers, and t-shirt were all covered with dirt. Rudi walked over to me. Neither one of us spoke for a few moments. Then he said, "I've broken with Baba, but I'm going to experiment with his techniques for a year or so. I'm going to use you as the guinea pig."

"Thanks for telling me," I said. "How deep should I dig this ditch?"

"There are many elements of magic I want to explore," he went on, "and you're one of the few students I have who can survive Baba's methods of teaching. You also need training in this. It will help you in your future life."

He walked away from me, looking more like a phantom from a dream than a living person. His feet barely touched the ground.

"Next year should be very interesting," I said to myself and took a deep breath.

Rudi once told me that he lived in my heart; he said that I should look for him there. He also told me that he would demand of me things I would never demand of myself. But finding him in my heart is often like a game of hide-and-seek. Sometimes I see him there sitting on a lotus flower in golden light. Mostly I'm just walking through a dark tunnel paneled with mirror images of myself — some recognizable, but many are mask-like visions created by my fragmented mind.

Rudi makes right and wrong seem like they have no place on earth. His logic transcends any rational thinking I can conjure up in my mind. "The guru is consciousness," he had said to me in his store, "and consciousness is life in all its manifestations. Don't ever judge it! Witness it! Learn from it and go on!"

My eyes close and I take a short nap, and in a dream, I'm walking on a dark and deserted street in a town I don't recognize. A blind man walks toward me. The sound of his tapping cane echoes off the buildings. "Who are you?" I ask. He continues to walk without paying me any mind. "Wait!" I cry out, "I've got questions to ask you." "Only fools come out this late at night. Only fools chase the wisdom of a blind man." "But the fog?" I ask him, "What about the fog?" "The plane will crash," he says in a shrill voice. "No!" I cry out to him as I awaken from my short nap and see the dense blanket of fog rolling over our plane.

The altimeter reads thirty-six hundred feet.

My mind weaves its way in and out of the past, present, and future, and is never quite sure which reality is pertinent to its existence. My mind is determined to drive me crazy. It's a prophet pontificating on the disconnectedness of all things.

"Children need love, not dogma," Rudi once said to me after we came out of a movie. "Parents that insulate children snuff the creative spirit out of them. The last thing a child needs or wants are lectures on right living. They're going to make mistakes, get into trouble, and 'blow it' at least a thousand times. A loving parent gives them space to learn about life, a loving parent will be there for them in both good and bad times, and never judges them or puts them down. It's best to send children away from home when they're eighteen years-old; it's best not to hold on to them or protect them against life. They're going to get beat up anyway. A parent might as well love them and let experience be their teacher. Children are very close to God and the innocence they bring into the world is lost when they grow up..."

I kiss Rudi's hand.

"Simplification preserves energy and allows it to shift onto a higher level," Rudi continues to dictate.

Simplification is a concept almost impossible for me to understand, I think. But listen to Rudi; listen to him and learn. Look for a shaft of light — a star, the earth...nothing! No moon, streetlight! Nothing!

"How are we doing?" I ask Beau.

"Fine," he answers.

Nothing's fine and nothing's forever, I think.

The day after I graduated from The New School's college program, I brought Rudi my diploma and asked him, "What wonderful thing is going to happen to me?" "Get a Master's degree," he replied, "and I want you to stop teaching our spiritual work." In one fell swoop, he forced me to continue college and took away from me the only thing in my life that had any value. I didn't say a word. I walked out of his store, went to the meditation room and sat before the altar, working hard on myself to keep from crying. I went deep inside to find an answer. Swami Nityananda came out of my heart and sat on the altar. "What has Rudi done to you?" he asked rhetorically. "If you get a Master's degree, it means Rudi's got to take full responsibility for your spiritual growth the next two years. He's got to give you everything. By taking away your teachings, he's pruned an unhealthy tree, rid you of your position in life and given you the opportunity to grow in an organic way." A rush of warm energy passed through my heart. I saw Rudi's smiling face peering out at me. I got up from the meditation, went back to his store, gave him a big hug and said, "thank you."

"I didn't think you'd get it this quickly," he responded and hugged me back. "Just remember, Stuart, that everything in nature is rooted," he went on. "But people in their tense, neurotic, pressure-filled lives lose their balance and forget how necessary foundation is. A tree doesn't skip around the orchard. It grows in place, sheds its leaves, re-grows them, and gracefully surrenders to the seasonal changes."

Then why does simplicity keep eluding me, I think.

"People resent change," Rudi went on. "It terrifies them. Even change for the better. Though they're starved for spiritual nourishment, though they want to love and be loved, though they want to be happy, they refuse to take the necessary steps to help themselves. They accept watered-down situations, answers that pacify egos, and relieve discomfort. It's like taking a shit. The next day you've got to go to the toilet again."

Somehow, society's notion of joy has little to do with what is perceived to be reality, I think. My eyes are closed and I don't want to open them to look into the swirling black clouds that have blanketed our plane. Somehow, simplicity's been knocked out of kids at an early age. People's eyes are filled with pain, and the rules of life, the commandments in religious texts are toy blocks in a kindergarten that have no practical place in the world.

"Happiness is the goal of all human striving," Rudi said once to me on a walk we took in the West Village. "If I think about it...if I try to find another goal...the world turns hopelessly absurd."

I don't want to think about it, because every time I dwell on why people suffer, I realize how quickly my dreams were snuffed out at an early age. I had to fight my way out of the Bronx; I had to fight to find Rudi.

Nothing ever came easy. It still doesn't come easy. But it does come. It took years of inner work, but finally my life changed. The impossible became possible, and I found a path to God. Rudi showed me that it took an exceptional person to see the spirit of God in today's world, an exceptional person to transform power, greed, and insensitivity into life–giving forces…

"I want you to go to Texas," Rudi said to me one day while we were sitting together on the second floor.

"To do what?" I asked him.

"Teach," he replied somewhat annoyed.

"But you told me that I'm no longer a teacher."

He looked at me for a moment and said, "I want you to go to Denton for three weeks to teach our work. I reinstate you. My students need you there." He took a sip of coffee and asked one of his disciples to see who rang the doorbell. Then he turned to me again: "At an early age," he said, "I asked a Tibetan lama how to get to God. 'Work,' he replied, 'and that'll bring more work. It's a snowball affect. As your capacity grows, your responsibilities will grow, until one day you work your way out of the world."

Three weeks in Denton turned into six months. On one of Rudi's frequent visits, while driving in the Denton countryside, I turned to him and said, "It's been a hell of a long three weeks." He replied, "You're on your fourth day." I immediately understood how time had no relevance, and how the earth could be created in six days, and how Methuselah lived 969 years. I laughed because I had never known three weeks could be six months and, at the same time, nothing more than a moment in time and space. Meanwhile, ashrams sprang up all over the state. I began university and prison programs, and businesses to support the meditation center. I thought I was working like a bullock, until that same day, on the ashram porch, Rudi told me I hadn't been working hard enough.

"What should I do?" I asked, a little bit in disbelief.

"Buy that building," he said pointing to a small shopping center next to the ashram.

"I've got six hundred dollars in the bank," I said.

"Anyone can do it with money," he replied and walked away.

The next morning I discovered the building was for sale, called the owners, and made an offer. Later that day I was told that the offer was accepted. The purchase of the building forced me to start three businesses and to learn to work twenty hours a day. I had a month to raise the down payment. If I could, a bank guaranteed that it would give me a mortgage. Rudi was right, anyone could do it with money, but I discovered that I had inner resources beyond anything I knew before and was capable of raising the money I needed to buy the building. A month later, the deal was finalized and the Denton ashram owned the building. I never gave a moment's thought to money before, other than for my basic needs. Buying the building taught me that I had inner resources I had never tapped.

There were times I'd work beyond the breaking point, and I'd hear Rudi say, "An extra effort is necessary to attain enlightenment." I'd go a little deeper into myself and find untapped energy, vast restorative powers, and the tiredness would disappear, and I'd have the strength to take on new projects. I'd say to myself, "Why set limitations? I'm the only reason I've not attained enlightenment as yet." When I complained to Rudi, he'd look at me as if I were a wingless fly. He'd ask me how long I'd been studying with him. "Six months," I'd answer, or "two years," or "three years." "If you have patience and endurance, you'll get to the other side of you. There's a wonderful Zen saying: 'Climb Mt. Fuji, O snail! But slowly, slowly.' Try to remember it the next time you're impatient."

I've got a long way to go, I think, but at least I'm on the path with someone who's already made the journey. I still need to learn how to navigate the whitewater rapids so deeply lodged in my mind.

It's strange living in Denton, Texas. Never, in all my life, could I envision myself in a small town that seems more a state of mind than anything else — a cultural wasteland when compared to New York. "A nice place to visit!" I once said to friends who had spent a weekend at the Denton ashram. "But I don't belong here."

Every Denton morning, a white two–story funeral parlor greets me as I leave home. It's just across the street — Schmidt's, Inc.

"I've buried the best Texans here," Mr. Schmidt bragged to me on a hot summer's day. "Simple folk, town fathers, mayors, lawyers, ranchers, doctors, generations of 'good ole boys.' Me and my pappy have laid them in the ground."

A parched ground, to be sure. A hot, sun baked ground with miles of grazing land, with two–lane blacktops winding in and out of forgotten towns, with thousands of mobile homes, and with old men sitting on general store porches swatting flies and mosquitoes, talking about the "good ole days," talking about oil and cattle, and about the "young'ns" that no longer respect the land.

Mr. Schmidt buries dead people in that land, and someday he'll bury me here if I don't finish up my three weeks in Denton, Texas, I think. I have only one option: that's to build an oasis in the desert, and Rudi's notion of "work bringing more work" is the best remedy for living in a small town in North Texas. It keeps me so busy I don't have time to worry about where I am and what I'm doing there.

"I feel like the last year of my life has prepared me for the understanding that expanded consciousness can only come through expanded Nothingness," Rudi dictates to Mimi.

I squeeze his hand because his words make so much sense to me. The less there is of me, the more there will be of God. I have to get out of the way...

I try to sleep again, but sleep is difficult because my mind is torn between spiritual thoughts and fear of the fog. I listen to my breathing and relax, and I remember Rudi hugging me this morning, and saying, "You've really changed, Stuart."

"Yes," I replied. "I feel it. I've discovered that I can be a vehicle for spiritual energy. I've ground my anger and possessiveness into tiny particles of dust, and truthfully, it's all very humbling."

"The ego is a real disease," he laughed. "It tears people apart."

"Especially when you accept it as all life has to offer."

Rudi laughed again. "So many people lock themselves in little boxes," he said. "We possess so little in life and ultimately have to surrender it all."

"I'm thankful for that."

"The crazy kid in you is growing up and finding a connection with God," he said. We walked into the second–floor living room of his house. He sat on a chair in half–lotus position, and I sat cross–legged at his feet. "A psychic channel connects the heart to the crown *chakra*," Rudi said to me, "and we can use that channel to offer gratitude directly to God. The root of that channel is the point where the heart *chakra* touches the spine. When you breathe into the heart, offer up joy and gratitude; try to expand the heart center so that the love that comes out of you is unconditional."

After we meditated together for about fifteen minutes, he uncrossed his legs, smiled and said, "People starve on lackluster spiritual diets. They need nourishment, not advice; and always remember you can be an A–plus Stuart or a B–minus Rudi. We're different people. We've got different chemistries. Spiritual energy won't flow through you like it flows through me. But that doesn't matter, because every one of us has something unique to offer.

"I've got no chosen heir," he went on. "I give to whomever wants to receive. It could be one person or a thousand people. Whoever's willing to work hard enough to get my teachings, and often, I think, if one person gets 'it,' my life will be a total success. If no one wants it, then I'll leave the *shakti* on a chair in a Chinese restaurant, and the next diner will get a jolt of *kundalini* he'll never forget."

The thought of my life prior to Rudi scares the shit out of me — a drugged-out brain, an eight-foot by eight-foot Spanish cell, insecurity by the truckload, and a skinny frightened kid who lived life like a nerve ending exposed to the elements. The word "nothing" meant failure to me then, and now it means there's room inside myself for spirit. I won't go back to that crippled life, not if it has to cost me everything. It's one thing to lust after God, but another to know how to get there.

The fog is getting thicker as I look out of the airplane window. The altimeter reads 2500 feet.

I'm not afraid of life or death, I think. I often laugh at them. I see them walking hand in hand on the streets of Manhattan. I spent too much time hiding from both life and death until Rudi taught me that they are one and the same thing. As a child, time and space stretched before me like an unbreakable rubber band. I felt invincible, godlike, and I believed death had no reality in my sphere of being. Then my father died, and death's tentacles wrapped themselves around every part of my mind and body. I cried and cried until there were no more tears. I had no idea where I was headed or what was the purpose of my life. Before my father's death, none of that mattered. His death made me realize that something was missing in most people's lives. I wanted to find it before I left the world. I didn't want to live like a mechanical toy. I questioned hundreds of people, but received very few answers. I read book after book, but always felt empty. That was before Rudi, and that still scares the shit out of me.

"You see, nothing's real, Stuart," Rudi said. We were eating blintzes in a Second Avenue dairy restaurant. "Look around you. It's a transient world filled with illusion — a dream, Stuart, a merry-go-round that never stops. It has everyone chasing things that have no substance. People refuse to internalize their energy, they refuse to get spiritual training and build lives that are strong enough to withstand tension and pressure. I mean, how much success do people really need? How much power, fame, and money? After a while, it gets silly. I remember seeing Swami Nityananda in a loincloth. He slept on a potato sack, and his entire body emanated light and love and spirituality. The thought that someday I, too, can live simply, that thought alone inspires me to do God's work. The world's not mine or yours or any one else's. It's a manifestation of spiritual energy, and whatever we possess one day will have to be surrendered. The most ambitious and greedy bloodsucker will eventually come to realize that no one can own the Infinite. The greatest treasure on earth is in the human heart, and once it opens, and stays open, then all questions become irrelevant. People can love each other and breathe easily.

"There are seven basic *chakras* in a human being," he went on. He asked the counterman to bring him a cup of coffee. "They are located in different parts of the body. Each of them is connected to the spine, and each of them is a direct link to God or Higher Energy in the Universe. People assume that meditation is an esoteric or occult practice that spaces one out, not realizing that meditation is simply a technique of repairing a dysfunctional system that will just get worse unless we do something about it. We're all like broken–down cars that need to go to the shop. The first cycle in meditation has more to do with learning to be human than becoming spiritual. As the mind gets quiet, as the throat, heart, and navel *chakras* open, we discover such human traits as compassion, forgiveness, love, and understanding, and our wholeness of person transforms itself into spiritual energy. That transformation takes place in the sex *chakra*; then energy flows to the base of the spine, activates the *kundalini*, which in turn rises to the crown *chakra*, opens it, and allows the soul force of a human being to pass into the cosmos. A spiritual life begins with the second cycle of energy; it begins when energy flows from the cosmos into the forehead, opening the third eye, and then on to the other *chakras*. In each *chakra* psychic and spiritual forces are awakened. They become part of consciousness, part of our everyday lives. It takes about seven years for the second cycle to begin and a lifetime for the seven cycles to complete themselves and for us to attain enlightenment and be permanently with God. The seventh cycle usually comes at the time of death."

He stopped talking for a moment, finished his coffee, asked the counterman for the check, paid it, and we walked back to his store. I told him that I needed to spend some time meditating. He just smiled and said that he'd see me later.

In the meditation room at the ashram, I sat cross-legged on the floor just in front of a picture of Rudi. I focused my mind and breathed deeply into the heart and navel *chakra,* and from that point on I saw only light and color, and the OM sound vibrated at the core of my being. I went into a deep trance and I asked God to take me further on the journey...

It's crazy to be wearing a light jacket, I think after I open my eyes and look out the airplane window. It's a February Indian Summer, perhaps an early spring, and the world's climates are changing, but it could be ten degrees outside tomorrow. I take Rudi's hand, squeeze it, and breathe once again into my navel *chakra*.

There's nothing to fear, I think, nothing to fear, "If only my mind could let go. If only...

"You'll never need another teacher," Rudi said to me one afternoon in his store.

"Sometimes I feel like I'm just learning to crawl," I replied.

"It's a beginning," he said. "A tomato needs to ripen on the vine. If we pick it early, it'll be sour and inedible. Vegetable gardens don't just grow. Their soil needs plowing, composting, seeding, mulching, and weeding, and above all, a healthy garden needs care, love and patience. Human beings are no different. They ripen on a karmic vine. I think it's better to offer God ripe fruit than a couple of fifty-cent hamburgers that'll mess up the internal workings of the universe. I think that tomatoes taste best ripe, and that time, patience, and deep spiritual work can make tender the thickest of human hides. We all eat and are being eaten, and if we ripen, if we're succulently overflowing with love, it'll be a joy for God to pluck us from our karmic vine.

"People are emotionally and mentally constipated," he went on. "What they need is a good dose of spiritual Drano to cleanse their psychic pipes."

What I need is a Laurel and Hardy movie to make me laugh till my sides ache, I think. I look out the plane window and see only black clouds. The altimeter reads 2200 feet and Beau is sitting there without saying a word. Sometimes I feel like I'm living halfway up a cosmic mountain. I can see neither the summit nor the base, and all I have is Rudi's wisdom to get me to the top. Sometimes I feel as if I'm living in a divine cartoon in which I'm cast as a "seeker after truth"; sometimes I wonder if I'll ever get off the mountain, or even if I want to get off the mountain...

"Everyone has *chakras,*" Rudi said. We were sitting together in his store. He cut a pear into four slices and gave me one. "The real mystery is why no one uses them, why people aren't willing to work hard enough on themselves to build a connection to God. An ashram is a place to work the psychic muscles and keep them from atrophying, just as physical muscles will atrophy if we don't use them, as the mind, liver and heart will atrophy if they're not used.

"The *chakra* below the navel," Rudi went on, "is the power source in a human being. The Japanese call it the *Hara*, the Chinese and Koreans, the *Tan–t'ien.* If a human being centers his mind in the navel *chakra*, the mind acts like a surgical instrument and opens the foundation of their being. People too often run from life, but no matter where they run, life's tendency is to find them and bite them in the ass. So it's best to stay put and build a strong inner life that will serve one no matter what is going on in the world..."

"In a little while, we'll pass through this," Beau whispers to me. I come out of my reverie.

No doubt, I think. Then I close my eyes and imagine myself riding headless on a motorcycle on a dark country road.

"They say God is love and that love is all around us," Rudi said in one of his talks following a meditation class. "They say it so much that it's become trite, and we forget how profound this truth is that appears on every church and synagogue bulletin board. But God is love and the love of God lives in every human heart. That love is the language of God on earth. The lotus flower blooms on muddy water. It's also a symbol of Buddhism; and once people learn to keep their hearts open, once they are grateful for what life brings them, they are no different than the lotus flower. They've learned to transform all their garbage into a spiritual life.

"The *chakras* are like petals on a flower," Rudi continued to speak after the meditation class, "one within the other, forming a *mandala* connected to a stem that's rooted in the foundation — the heart beneath the throat and the navel supporting everything. When we meditate it's like playing in a one–man band because each *chakra* is necessary to the opening of the others and each a link to spiritual enlightenment, and we have to make sure that they are all open. Just as we'd tune a musical instrument before playing it, we're responsible for tuning the *chakra* system. We have to make sure that our minds are quiet and that we feel gratitude; we have to make sure that our spiritual instrument is ready to be played. The moment we take ourselves for granted, the entire process stops. They say that "familiarity breeds contempt," and that holds true for meditation practice. You cannot assume anything. You have to work for many years to fine tune your instrument and prepare it to receive spiritual energy."

When I'm around you, Rudi dear, my mind gets quiet, my heart opens, and I feel inner strength…

"The state of expanded consciousness is produced by surrendering the tensions that bind and restrict our physical mechanism from expressing the power of creation," Rudi dictates to Mimi.

When I'm around you, a spiritual fire burns my tension...

"Ordinarily, the mind's excesses destroy creativity, forcing it to turn back on itself," Rudi continued after a meditation class, "and polarize everything. It creates a rational and self–righteous prison of ideas and beliefs that conflict with other people's perceptions of life. It torments us with Medusa–like creations that run amok in our thoughts. But the mind is also a great tool when we learn to use it consciously. It is a super–fine surgical instrument that can cut away emotional and mental blocks that keep us from connecting with God. Real knowledge is the end product of years of spiritual work. It transforms complexity and complication into a simple, clear and practical vision of life."

He sees past the illusion that blinds the rest of us, I think. How has he learned to transform everything he touches into spirituality? How does he make it look so easy? I look at the instrument panel and see that the altimeter reads 1600 feet. I don't know what to make of all this, but Rudi is in the back seat. He's dictating to Mimi. Nothing can happen…

"The one thing I do that virtually no other spiritual teacher does," Rudi said to me in the living room of his apartment — it was 6:50 PM and we were about to go downstairs to the meditation hall — "is teach technique. It's one thing to talk about spiritual enlightenment and another to teach people an exercise that makes it possible for them to attain it. I'm a technician, Stuart," he laughed, "that's all I do is teach technique." He put his finger on my forehead, and I felt jolts of energy moving from the base of my spine to the top of my head. The entire room filled up with white light. When I came out of the trance, he looked at me with a smile on his face and said, "The parameters of ordinary knowledge limit consciousness to something that resembles a sailboat on a windless sea where movement, change, vitality, and a profound spiritual force virtually cease to exist. It's the unknown quantity that transforms the human into the divine; it's the unknown quantity that inspires creativity in men. The marriage of disciple and guru in an eternal struggle to find

God is the most important marriage on earth, and it's never easy. Both must surrender and both must be one–pointed and both must realize that it's a marriage ceremony performed by God. Its purpose is spiritual enlightenment. Both guru and disciple must remember that the real battlefield of truth is inside themselves and not with each other. Both must remember that the only thing separating them from God is their own unwillingness to work hard enough to achieve enlightenment. It's their own fault if one or the other doesn't make the grade."

On the other side of me is my connection to God, I think, and every moment that I spend with Rudi teaches me how to slay myself.

My eyes are closed and I feel Rudi's moist hand in mine.

"I want you to teach your first class," Rudi said to me in the middle of a poker game at 11:45 AM, and fifteen minutes before a meditation class at Big Indian.

"Today?"

"Yes."

"But class is in fifteen minutes...we're in a poker game...and?" Then I laughed and said to him, "You always do this to me."

"Go take a shower."

I dropped my cards and ran upstairs to the bathroom. "There are no bad students," I remembered Rudi saying as the water hit my body. "Just teachers that don't know what they are doing." Just surrender, Stuart. Let go of yourself. "Never for a moment think you're doing it," Rudi kept repeating in my thoughts. "That's the quickest way to end your spiritual life."

The child is growing up. The child is taking a step to help free his guru...

There were a hundred students in the Big Indian ashram meditation room, all expecting Rudi to teach a noonday class. When I sat down on the altar, I sensed a different vibration in the room, from surprise to elation to let down, jealousy and gratitude — a vibration that passed through me and was burned up in the meditation class. I focused deep inside myself and thanked God for having given me the opportunity to serve my teacher. The forty–five–minute class felt more like a few seconds. It passed by before I even got a handle on what I was doing.

"Next summer at Big Indian," Rudi said to me after the class with a big smile on his face, "first I'll teach, then you'll teach, then we'll show cartoons." It was a great relief to know that Bugs Bunny could replace me as a teacher of meditation. I never took my position on the altar too seriously.

On the other side of me, I think and turn to the back seat of the airplane, look Rudi in the face — there's my connection to spirit…

"It's God flowing through us," he continues to dictate to Mimi. Rudi's warm hand fills mine with love, "and showing us how we are connected to Him…

You gave birth to me, I think. You're my father and mother.

"…as the expression of Higher Will," Rudi dictates.

Slowly, I'm learning the ways of God in the world…

"And a deeper sense of surrender..."

"Oh! My God!" Beau cries out. I turn around. From a dark cloud mass, a primordial mountain appears that destroys our plane…

"Rudi's dead," Beau whispers to me.

I kneel and place my lips on my teacher's, breathe into his mouth and massage his heart. "It can't be."

"He's gone," Beau says again.

I sit on a cold mountain rock, the plane strewn around me — a wing here, a fuselage there, a propeller leaning against a tree, the cold night air chilling my joints and bones...down I go into the depths of my being where fear cuts through fog and mist and tiny lights glitter on far away mountain peaks. "But where am I?" I think, "perhaps a place so secret that only my inner self knows of its existence."

"Six," I say to Beau through the haze. He puts his arm around me. A warm sensation trickles through my body. Beau's face moves in and out of focus. "Six," I say again, not knowing why the night and fog came so quickly, covering the mountains, the sky, the stars and the moon, not knowing if I'd ever see Rudi again. "I hear a six year-old child crying 'Rudi, Rudi,'" I say with tears streaming down my face, and blood pouring from my mouth. But it's all a dream; soon I'll awaken, and the flight will continue towards a small town near Albany.

That's how it ended…on a mountaintop in upstate New York. That's also how it began: life and death, two intertwined serpents. The past died on the mountain and the future rose up and spit fire in my face — a future coiling and uncoiling, leaving me groping in the dark.

Then a light sleep…

I dream of a large, toothless face spitting blood on my jacket, of a cold winter's night spent on a mountaintop, of Beau, Mimi and myself huddled around a fire, and Rudi lying dead near the remnants of a plane. That's how it began and ended...in a dream, three blind specters seated beneath the stars, three lost souls: day and night no more, life and death no more, and the sound of Rudi's name echoing everywhere.

When I was six years–old, I'd lie in bed at night and listen to a voice chant "Rudi" in my thoughts — night after night, month after month, it lulled me to sleep.

"Rudi."

His name rushed through my mind like a brook down a mountainside into a black pit raging with half–thoughts and memories. In the other room, my father talked.

"Two months in New Hampshire," he said.

"It's good for hay fever," Mother responded.

"The kids'll enjoy it."

I listened to a high–pitched electronic sound accompanied by a distant voice that chanted "Rudi, Rudi." A cat meowed in the backyard. A garbage can rattled. The ceiling's faint whiteness shimmered above and the voice grew louder.

Nighttime's longer when you're six years–old, especially if you spend the dark hours listening to aberrations.

"Bethlehem, New Hampshire."

"It'll cost five hundred dollars for the whole summer," Father said.

Bethlehem? I thought. Nativity? Was Jesus born in New Hampshire… in the White Mountains?

If only the plane would stop hitting the mountain and the pale white face stop spitting blood.

"The Messiah will come when we rebuild the Holy Temple of Israel," my Grandfather once said.

But how can we rebuild the Holy Temple while living in the Bronx...?

If only...?

When the voice stopped, I slept soundly, not caring about aberrations, cats' meows, or the plans of my parents. I slept for nineteen years until the voice and its body commingled and my search for a spiritual teacher ended.

And now, the mountain's taken him. Once again, I'll have to be satisfied with unhinged voices. But the mountain's a dream, isn't it? It's woven from threads of light and darkness. The plane's a dream, isn't it? My numb and aching body is a dream?

Rudi.

The silence cuts deep into a six year–old child; a primordial mountain has made everything different.

It took nineteen years for me to find Rudi and one second to lose him. Now, I'll have to look for my spiritual teacher again, but this time in divine and mysterious places. From now on the song of Rudi will be sung in my heart. I see him sitting there: he's smiling, laughing, guiding me, and sharing his love and wisdom. Rudi, Rudi — you've disappeared from the earth, my love, you are hiding from me at the very center of my own being…

"New Hampshire's no place for a kid from the Bronx," I say to Beau. He shakes his head, and pats me on the shoulder. "You'll be alright," he says. "The bleeding will stop."

But the song of "Rudi" doesn't.

I'm asleep once again and in the middle of a dream: a dark whirlwind of a cloud with angelic, orange–robed lamas flying in and out of the mist, wide–eyed, beatific faces and ethereal shapes suspended in the air, a mountain moving upwards into the cosmos. At its base, mendicant *Saivite* monks are in prayer. A plane flies into the dark mass and I hear a voice whisper: "Rudi's dead. He's dead!" Once again, a plane flies into the blackness. It doesn't come out.

The voice whispers: "The plane crashed. He died on the mountain-top. He put his life into you."

"Yes, I know," I reply. Then I wake up with a gasp only to see Rudi's body lying in front of me on the ground…

In Memoriam 8/2/11

A small plaque sits beside the remaining wreckage of the plane that came down in the Catskill Mountains of New York above North Lake.
Photo courtesy of Claudio Musajo

RUDI PICTURES

USE →
CROSSWALK
TO TERMINAL

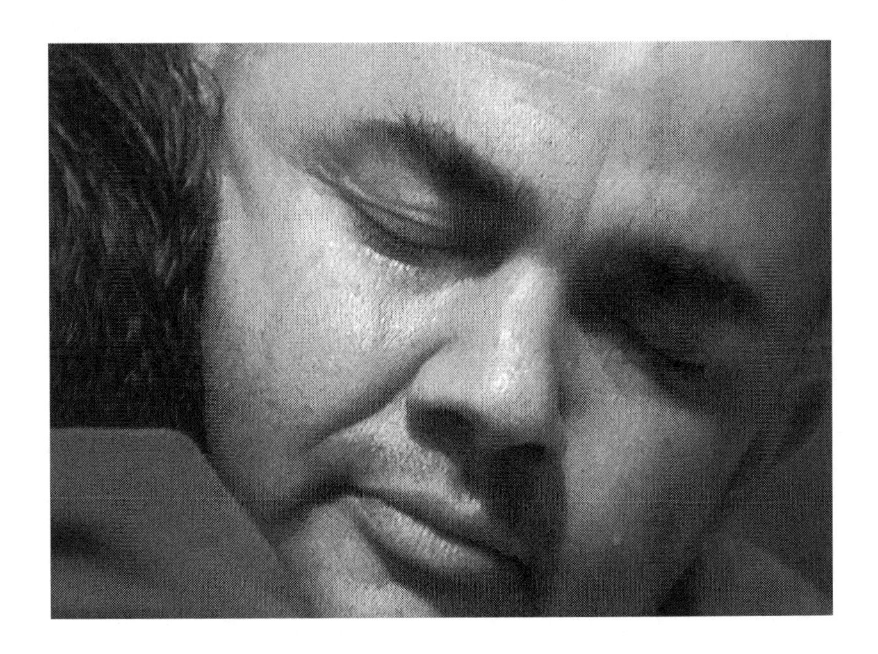

CAPTAIN
KUNDALINI

Afterward

Rudi's passing presented a whole new set of problems for me. I had to make serious decisions about the life I was leading and the future. He had told me many times that the best gift you can give your guru is to develop an inner life that's so strong it connects you directly to God. All I wanted was a spiritual life and I discovered that it was incumbent on me to build within myself an unshakable connection with Higher Creative Energy in the Universe.

I was living in Denton, Texas at the time of the crash, grateful to be running a meditation center that Rudi had started a year earlier. My sole purpose in running that center was to devote every moment of my time to spiritual growth. Nothing in me believed that Denton was the best fit for my life, but given the opportunity to nurture people and serve Higher Energy in the Universe, I took full advantage of the situation and spent my time there working on myself. It turned out that the ashram in Denton was a blessing. If nothing else, it taught me patience; it also taught me to complete cycles, to love people, to learn from them and to use that learning to get closer to God. Rudi had sent me there for three weeks. It took nine years to complete those three weeks.

When I returned to New York City, the fit was better for me, and I began to see Rudi's teachings spread around the world. I would travel to Berlin, Athens, Paris, Jerusalem, São Paulo, Brazil, and many other cities in the United States where meditation centers had sprung up. The work was overwhelming, but wonderful, and every day, I felt stronger and more capable of doing God's service on earth. No matter what tensions manifested in my life, Rudi's teachings showed me how to transform them into spiritual energy.

I discovered that enlightened people don't even know they are enlightened. They just live that way. Their hearts are open, there's joy and love inside them, and their interaction with other people is rooted in compassion. They have evolved to a place in themselves where they are capable of living in the moment.

My meditation work shifted. The struggle no longer had to do with the attainment of some mystical goal, but the simple use of every life experience to get me closer to my own humanity. It was a great revelation to me when I discovered that *human beings* have spiritual lives, not necessarily wise men dressed in robes or theologians and people with vast intellects that can talk for hours on arcane mysteries in the universe. All that means is that people have to learn to live with their hearts open, with joy inside them, and with compassion for the human race and its boundless suffering. Finding people who can live that way is almost as difficult as finding the Holy Grail. But, every human being is born with tools (mind, breath, *chakras*, and will) that can be used to master their inner selves. The problem is always learning how to do it.

It's been thirty-eight years since Rudi took his Samadhi, and never for a day have I forgotten what a blessing it was to have spent six years with him. His teachings not only saved my life, they paved a road for me that led to extraordinary life adventures. In my wildest imaginings, I could never have conjured up the journey I have taken and the guidance I've received on that journey from Rudi. It is with the utmost respect and gratitude that I dedicate this book to him.

THE DANCING MAN

I was away at college when word came that my father was ill. The doctors had said that he might not live out the week; I should return home as soon as possible. I threw together some belongings and took a train back to New York. At Grand Central Station, I descended to the platform and walked through the crowded terminal to the subway. I was so immersed in my thoughts and fears that I scarcely remembered the ride from Manhattan to the Bronx. Only when I entered my old neighborhood did my trancelike state fade.

The familiar tenement buildings, the streets teeming with pedestrians and shoppers, with kids and parents dragging kids, the magical arena of shops selling everything from yard goods, haberdashery, smoked fish, dried fruit and nuts, to men's and women's clothing, delicatessen meats, pickles, spices, and a thousand other things that drew crowds to the street; the odors wafting out of stores, the vendors hawking their goods, all revived childhood memories of the Bronx I knew so well. I listened to scraps of conversation, saw fleeting images of half-familiar faces, stopped and gazed and wondered at the memories flitting through my brain.

I walked slowly along 174th Street to Bryant Avenue to the tenement in which my parents lived. Nearly tripping over an old man dressed in a torn and dirty suit, his fly was open, his face unshaven and his body swayed beneath the weight of each step — an old man growling at me as he tried to cross the street.

"Got a nickel?" he asked. "Help an old man get his next drink." He laughed and scratched himself. "Just a nickel, son," he called after me as I walked away. "There's no God in this world," he muttered. "No compassion!"

"Your father's been in the hospital for two weeks," my mother said.

She sat at the kitchen table peeling an apple. Dark rings were under her eyes and her face was puffed and raw from crying. "It's not good, Joshua. He lies in bed shaking. He doesn't know me anymore. The doctors keep saying I have to be patient. For what? His death?" She started to cry and I put my arms around her. "You have to go see him," she said. "Before that terrible fever came, he asked for you."

"I'll go now," I said.

"I don't know what I'm going to do," she said. "We've been married more than twenty-five years." She cried in my arms until she fell asleep. I carried her to the bed and laid her on it. "It will be all right," I whispered as I spread a blanket over her. Then I walked out of the bedroom.

Death seemed so remote to me. It was something that happened outside my circle of acquaintance, something I read about in the newspapers. I had seen actors suffer its finality only to return again in new movies or television shows; I had heard people speak of the death of some distant relative or some friend; I had even had youthful fantasies about which of my parents would die first — and it always turned out to be the one I was angry with at the time. But death had never touched me. Now my father was dying. We would never again take long walks together, or knock a baseball around the diamond, or go to the fights, or just sit at the kitchen table. This simple reality was more than I could fathom.

The hospital lay beyond a tangle of unfamiliar streets. They were full of activity and reminded me of my public school days: teenagers lounged around the street corners, young boys played stickball in the schoolyards, and children played tag or kick-the-can. I turned down a street that was littered with trash. The black tar was torn up and the tenements had been burned or were collapsing, and small groups of men were busy shooting craps. A huge rat ran along the curb and jumped into a garbage can, and a sparrow was perched on a street lamp above me. It pierced the silence of the tension-filled block with a song that brought a smile to my face. I tried not to think about my father.

The hospital's lobby was busy with crowds of nameless and faceless people moving to and from the elevators. The clerk at the information desk told me that my father was in room 426. She gave me a visitor's pass and pointed to the elevator, where I found groups of doctors and nurses chatting calmly with each other. There were also many nervous people like myself visiting friends and family that were in-patients. When the elevator arrived, I squeezed in and took it to the fourth floor.

The very thought of my father dying drove me to blank out any image of the man who was so full of life the last time I saw him. None of it could be true. One's father doesn't just die like that. At least, he has to give some notice.

Many nurses were scurrying about the fourth floor and others had gathered at a centralized desk — some were laughing and gossiping, drinking cokes and iced tea, yet others busy answering phone calls or doing paper work. I asked a nurse where I could find room 426. She pointed to it and told me that my father's doctor had just checked in on him. He was coming out of the room and I could talk to him if I wanted. "Hurry up," she said. "He's got lots of patients to see." When I introduced myself, the doctor greeted me with a soft and compassionate voice and told me that my father suffered from acute peritonitis and an extreme malfunction of the colon. His chances of survival were bleak. I asked him if I could go in.

"Whenever you wish," he said with a detached sadness. He shook my hand and walked away.

His room was like every other hospital room — green walls, television set, and a couple of armchairs. There were curtains around the bed, and when I separated them, I saw my father lying beneath the covers. His face was pale and drawn, and his eyes were sunken and dark in their sockets. He was feverish and shook beneath the covers, mumbling what sounded to me like a primitive chant. Saliva dripped from the corner of his mouth onto his pajama top. I sat down on a chair by his bed.

"Dad," I whispered. "Can you hear me?" He continued to shake and didn't respond, "He's a good man," I thought. "He loved his family and took care of it. Why this? No one ever told me about this!"

"Can you hear me, Dad?" I said again and touched his arm. He did not respond. "He can't die like this," I thought. But he lay on his bed in the throes of a relentless fever. "I never told him that I love him," I said aloud to myself. "We didn't really know one another. We did things together, went places, argued, laughed, cried, but I don't know who he is. We're like two strangers sitting at the edge of a cliff." I walked over to the window and parted the curtains. A pigeon landed on the ledge. It looked into the room, turned and flew away.

"Is it too late?" I asked myself. "Can I get across the bridge?" A helpless sensation crept over me. There was a wisp of cloud in the sky, and I watched it make strange configurations as it moved above the city. Across the street some teenage boys were taunting a pretty girl.

"Joshua," I heard a voice whisper. "Joshua, come here."

My father lay quietly on his bed. His fever had subsided, and there was a faint smile on his lips. I walked over to him. "It's wonderful to see you," he said. His voice was weak but remarkably clear. I sat down next to him, took his hand in mine and kissed it. His eyes were filled with tears and his touch gentle. "It's only the beginning," he said. "I have finally let go." He closed his eyes again and fell into a light sleep. His hands were warm and his lips pale, his breath was easy and rhythmic, and beads of sweat stood out on his forehead, and I looked, as if for the first time, at his unshaven face, the contour of his chin, and the hair on his chest.

"Every moment is now precious," I thought, "and I can no longer take his presence for granted." Then I ran my fingers through his hair and over the outline of his face.

"Why has it taken me so long to understand that I love you," I thought. "Thank God we have been given these last moments; thank God we can sit together without anger and fear."

The deep silence of the room was interrupted by his rhythmic breathing — a warm current of energy flowed from his hand into mine, and I never felt closer to him.

He continued to doze. From time to time, he would open his eyes and smile at me. There was now a child–like sweetness about him. There was quiet resolution in his face and it spoke of his freedom from the burden of living. He opened his eyes, smiled at me and squeezed my hand. The barrier that stood between us for so many years — a wall we had erected which neither of us had ever crossed — was all but gone.

"I love you, Joshua," he said softly. "It's easy now. I've cut the moorings and the river isn't as wide as I thought it would be. There's a time when we have to let go of life and meet the unknown. Strangely enough, I feel no fear." Then he smiled at me and said, "It's foolish to contest the inevitable." He closed his eyes. I wiped the sweat from his brow and a few moments later he spoke again. "It's almost as if I'm seeing the world like a child," he said in barely a whisper. "I recognize its vastness, and understand how useless it is to try to control things. I'm at peace, Joshua, something I've wanted for a long time."

He slept again. A nurse came in to check his vital signs, and after she left, my father awakened, and was pleased to see me sitting there.

"As soon as the doctor told me that I was dying," he said, "something changed in me. My mind cleared itself of static that had always been there, and I was able to take a good look at the world around me. For the first time I understood how much of life I had missed. Do you know that I can't tell one tree from another, and I know nothing about flowers or insects or even much about cats and dogs? I can't distinguish one cloud from another or how they announce the weather. I've lived like a blind man, Joshua. My view was circumscribed by my narrowest preoccupations."

He closed his eyes again, took a few deep breaths and fell silent for a few moments.

"The secret is to live moment by moment, day by day," he said after opening his eyes. "It doesn't have to make sense. That may be what we're born here to learn. I once believed that there was a rational design to life, that its complexities could be explained. But answers that made sense at one moment were irrelevant the next. I'll be dead soon, and I know less now than I did at your age." He grew pensive and tried to find the words to express his deepest feelings. "I wanted to love you and your mother and do more for you, but I busied myself with my own interests and left no time for the people closest to me. It seems that all of my activity stemmed from the fear of the unknown. I was incapable of making peace with myself and had little or no clarity when it came to understanding my life." Then he gently squeezed my hand. "I'm grateful, Joshua, that we can love one another in these last moments." I leaned over and kissed him as he dropped into a deep and sudden sleep.

"Thank you," I said. Still holding his hand, I slumped into my chair and also fell asleep.

What follows is an account of the dreams I had while sleeping by my father's bed. I have taken the liberty of connecting them so that the current of thought and vision makes a continuous narrative. In the darkness of my sleep, I returned to my childhood and the pleasure I once took in the performance of a person we called The Dancing Man. My youth was a carefree time in which the laughter was pure and the friendships were unconditional, and The Dancing Man was integral to my growing up. He would perform at seven every evening beneath a streetlamp at the top of a hill on Bryant Avenue between 173rd and 174th Streets. My friends and I sat in awe as he leaped and spun and did miraculous things. We memorized his every step. We laughed and cried with him and always wondered about the face behind the white mask he wore and never took off. How many times had I shouted with the rest of the audience:

"Take off the mask. Let us see your face. Who are you?"

Although the rest of his costume always changed, the white mask remained the same.

The crowd had already assembled at the top of the hill. Early evening shadows blanketed the tenements, and their lighted windows revealed many people waiting patiently to see The Dancing Man. The men were in undershirts and shorts and the women in shapeless smocks — with vacant eyes and pale faces, they sat on fire escapes and in window casements looking down on the streets. The tenement buildings leaned on each other like wounded soldiers returning from a war front, and cats and dogs climbed the steps between fire escape landings — some growling, others whining, all hungry and looking for food. A large crowd had gathered on the street — people of every age, from toddlers with their parents to octogenarians seated in a row of garden chairs. Some of the children played tag and others hide-and-seek, and an ice-cream truck dispensed vanilla and chocolate cones to customers trying to cool down in the summer's heat. When The Dancing Man appeared, the audience grew quiet, the games of the children stopped, and the sound of "hush" rippled through the air. Behind him, at the very top of the hill, there was a burned-out tenement building that made a dark and foreboding backdrop to his lamp-lit stage. It rose above us like the ruins of an ancient city.

He wore a rainbow-hued costume of colors that flowed from his chemise to his pantaloons. His face was covered with a white mask and he looked no different than I remembered him looking when I was a child.

Some of the children climbed on the shoulders of their parents. Others crawled between the legs of adults or pushed and shoved until they fought their way to the front of the crowd. There were many childhood friends among the onlookers and they stood out in a sea of unfamiliar faces.

"Joshua!" I heard a voice cry out. It was Rachel, my high school girlfriend waving to me. She was adjusting the Dancing Man's mask and picking lint off his chemise. I had started toward her, but stopped walking when The Dancing Man made a sign that the performance was about to begin. The audience clapped, the music commenced, and the crowded streets reverted to a pensive silence and everyone waited expectantly for him to dance.

He was an accomplished performer who used mime to transform his nimble self into a young girl walking gingerly down the street — a young girl who smiled and laughed, and stopped to listen to the songs of birds. She looked inquisitively into car windows, talked emphatically to a friend, opened an imaginary umbrella to shade herself from the encroaching moonlight, sucked on a lollipop and performed a number of pirouettes. She waved to someone in the distance, respectfully curtsied, and, as her body bent towards the ground, she noticed a flower growing out of a crack in the sidewalk. She got down on her knees and admired it. She sniffed it and touched it, and even spoke with it in her mute way. She called over a few members of the audience. They gathered around, and she pointed at the beautiful flower growing where nothing should normally grow.

His next performance was song and dance — almost like a scene from a Broadway musical, he tap-danced and belted out a love song that reminded me of Fred Astaire or Gene Kelly. Finally, he reverted to mime and, without saying a word, he spoke to sparrows, robins and imaginary pigeons that sat on his shoulders. He found beauty in unlikely places, but above all, he danced with a purity of spirit that stirred all who watched him.

When the music ceased playing, he raised his arms to the audience and bowed deeply. He gently lifted the imaginary flower from the crack in the sidewalk and gave it to a child seated on the curb. Then he disappeared into the tenement building behind him. The audience's wild applause and cries for more rang out above the rooftops, and I found myself so caught up in The Dancing Man's performance that I also wanted more. When I looked up and down the street for Rachel, she was gone. In her place, and standing on the exact spot on which the Dancing Man performed, a haggard old woman whose face was dark with mascara and rouge and who wore a tight skirt that clung to gnarled and crippled legs, cried out my name and beckoned me to come to her.

"Rachel," I said to myself. "Where are you?"

But Rachel was nowhere to be found, not in the crowd, nor on any of the fire escapes. She had disappeared.

"Joshua," the old woman shouted. "I know where to find Rachel. Come with me."

"Where?" I asked.

"Just come," she replied.

Compelled to see my old sweetheart, but not knowing where to look, I found the old woman's promise quite alluring. She was as twisted as the root of a tree, scabrous and ancient, and her voice had a bit of a growl in it. The moment I stepped towards her, the music began, and a midget exited the burned-out building and ran center stage. The whole thing appeared to be choreographed by some mystical force that drew me further into the dream.

"I need a volunteer," the midget cried out. He raised his hands in the air and demanded silence, "someone who wants to learn how to dance."

All the children raised their hands exuberantly, but he didn't choose any of them.

"Joshua," he said to me. "Would you like to learn to dance?"

"What're you talking about?" I replied.

"Dance, my friend, like you never dreamed it was possible to dance."

"Come on," I said. "I'm here for only a few days. My father's dying."

He shook my hand enthusiastically and told me his name was Osmond. "I'm his right-hand man," he said.

"Who?" I asked him.

"The Dancing Man," he replied. Then he wrapped his arms around my legs and held on to me for dear life.

"What are you doing?" I asked him. I tried to free myself, but couldn't.

"I've found a volunteer! I've found a volunteer!" he screamed at the top of his lungs, and all the people who had gathered around us cheered.

I tried to loosen the grip he had on my leg, but the more I resisted, the tighter it got. Osmond had dragged me beneath the streetlamp in front of a crowd of laughing and cheering people. They tossed confetti into the air, lit firecrackers and sparklers, and there was a festive air of celebration. Then Osmond let go of my leg and stood up. "The Dancing Man's getting old," he said in a serious voice. "He's going to retire soon. We need someone to replace him."

"Me?" I laughed. "Why me?"

"I don't know," Osmond replied, "but you're the one he pointed to."

"Joshua," I heard Rachel call out. She and the old lady stood together at the burned-out building's entrance. "Listen to him," she said. "He knows what he's talking about."

"Rachel," I called to her. "Wait."

But the moment I stepped in her direction, she and the gnarled old lady entered the charred and desolate-looking tenement and disappeared.

Osmond had long, disheveled brown hair and a wisp of beard, and he wore a colorful silk shirt and trousers and elfin-type red shoes that curled upwards and came to a point. He was part fool, part clown, and full-time representative of The Dancing Man to the public. He pulled out a scroll, untied the cord that bound it, and began to read. His voice was hoarse and grating.

"Legend has it that The Dancing Man first appeared three thousand years ago in the Middle East. He was a mendicant monk, and lived by a river on the outskirts of a tiny hamlet. His sole possession was a staff. When he danced, the village people came to marvel at the spirituality of his performances. Word spread throughout the country, and pilgrims came from far and near to watch. He taught the art of the dance to a disciple, and, in this way, his genius has been passed from generation to generation. There have been disciples in India, Eastern Europe, Spain, the Far East, and, now, in America. The mystery of his dance can be passed on only to a chosen successor. That person will appear when he is needed, and only he and he alone can master the art of The Dancing Man."

Osmond rolled up the parchment and The Dancing Man made another appearance. This time, he was dressed completely in black, but the same white mask covered his face. He came up to me, bowed, turned to the audience, and bowed again.

"In many ways, his dance is like the wind pushing its way over the mountains," Osmond said, "and its beauty is transcendent. He is your teacher, Joshua; watch him closely. If you learn well, you will dance as he does."

Osmond disappeared in the large convocation of people that had assembled and left me alone on stage with The Dancing Man. The lights, the applause, and the wide–eyed and expectant faces of onlookers confused me. They were all strangers, and I couldn't, for the life of me, understand why they continued to stare. All I wanted to do was return to the hospital; I wanted to sit at my father's bedside and leave this strange dream. I looked for Osmond, for Rachel, for any familiar face, but recognized no one — not even a member of my own family or an old friend from the neighborhood, not a familiar person stood on the crowded streets waiting for the Dancing Man to begin his performance. It wasn't a hostile audience, but one full of joy, innocence, and happy to witness the occasion — an audience that also stared at me with wide–eyed expectation.

The music swelled and the sublime movement of The Dancing Man dissolved my fear. His masked face moved in and out of my consciousness and multicolored strobes bathed the stage with fractured rays of light that were more rainbow–like than theatrical. At the center of all this was The Dancing Man, poised on one leg and completely balanced.

"The form of his dance," I heard Osmond whisper, "is a mystery. But it reminds one that all movement is sublime and that it's impossible to make sense out of any of this."

"It's just a dream," I replied.

"That's what you think," Osmond answered laughing.

"I came here to be entertained," I replied, trying to keep at bay deep anger that I felt because Osmond's answer was so vague. "I wanted to recapture my youth — a simple time, one full of joy — a time when The Dancing Man was just another street performer. He was once a clown and a mime, and I liked him because he made me laugh."

"Life is but a dream," Osmond's whimsical voice sang, *"and Joshua sailed on a boat that went to the moon."* Then he said with a laugh, "I don't think he ever wanted to return to the streets of the Bronx."

The Dancing Man's quick movements dazzled me and all I could see were fleeting images of his white mask; and the burned-out building that stood as a backdrop to the stage had transformed itself into an ark that housed a multitude of animals, birds, insects and people. My father peeked out from one of its windows. He motioned for me to come on board, but the moment I stepped towards him, the ark disappeared, the music stopped, and when I came out of my trance, I heard thunderous applause. The Dancing Man bowed and thanked the audience. Then he took my hand and led me into the door of the burned-out building.

"Where am I?" I asked, but received no answer. He bowed once again, turned his back on me, and disappeared like a fleeting specter into the shadows of the building's corridor.

"Don't try to understand," said Osmond, from behind me. "It's impossible, anyway. You'll waste a great deal of time and effort."

"I'm going mad," I said.

"A little," he replied with a smile. "You've created me and The Dancing Man and Rachel. Trust us. We'll guide you."

"All I want to do is relive a few joyous moments from my past."

"It's dead, Joshua. Let it go."

From the building's window, I could see the crowd breaking up and people walking down the hill.

"You can join them," said Osmond. "You just have to wake up."

"It's a good idea," I said. "I'm going to join them. I have no idea what I'm doing here."

"It's your choice," he replied.

"Osmond!" I said after having taken a few steps towards the building's exit. "I just came from the hospital where my father's dying. There's nothing I can do about it, and I'm frightened, for God's sakes, I'm really frightened. Can I speak with The Dancing Man?"

"Not yet," he replied.

"When?"

"I don't know."

Once again, I looked out of the window.

"Isn't it strange," Osmond continued in a soft voice. "They all suffer, yet so few of them understand the ground rules of life? They love The Dancing Man. They come here every evening to watch him. He lifts them up. Then they return to the ordinary struggles of their day."

His voice trailed off and I watched the crowd disperse — some of the people entered buildings, others turned left or right at street corners, others were lost to my sight as they walked through shadows that now blanketed the tenement buildings and sidewalks.

"The sight of my dying father scared me," I said, "but not the fact that he was near death, Osmond. That happens to everyone. What scared me was the way he lived in a world of false security and thought nothing could touch him. He hid behind walls he created to protect himself from life, and never, not for a moment, dared step into the unknown. What scared me the most was that he died before he ever truly lived."

"That is why you are here," Osmond said.

"But I don't know what is real or what is an illusion. This is a dream, isn't it? How can I learn anything from a dream?"

"It's an ass–backwards dream," Osmond said with a shrug, "but you can turn it around for yourself. You can kick it in the pants and ride on its shoulders, and if you remain here long enough, you will be infected by the vision of The Dancing Man."

"The what? I asked.

"Don't worry about it," he replied. "My instructions are to take you to see a man we call The Elder."

⁜ ⁜ ⁜

Osmond led me up a stairwell to the first floor of the building. Gas lamps and candles lit the hallway. Charred walls rose high above us and there were many exposed beams and two–by–fours, and all were covered with thick clumps of ash that periodically dropped to the floor. There was no glass in the building's windows, and to my surprise, I peered out at a panoramic view of trees, meadows, hills, and a river in the distance, with many people walking on a great lawn.

"Where are we?"

"It's the land of The Dancing Man," he said laughing. "It's your dream. You tell me, Joshua, because I don't know. But does it really matter? If you try to make sense of it, Joshua, you'll destroy all the possibilities."

"You've got to be kidding," I said.

"No, Joshua, because dreams slip through our thoughts the same way as wind moves through a forest," Osmond went on.

He told me in a furtive manner that dreams teach us about a world beyond our understanding. They are the artist's friend and the logician's enemy — a strange and mysterious place where we begin to take chances. We step out of a conceptualized box full of prefabricated ideas and notions and give our true self the room to create.

"I don't know why people want to understand everything," he said. "I suppose it's just insecurity or some compulsive need to control the forces of life. Isn't it strange how we worship the familiar, and how we need to be right all the time — as if there's a real winner when it comes to any kind of conflict?"

At the age of fourteen, Osmond had run away from a Sisters of Mercy orphanage where he had lived most of his life. He hid in vacant buildings and stole food and clothing to survive.

The nuns had always treated him like a favorite son. They were kind to him and had raised him from his infancy. They gave little parties for him, catered to his whims, tutored him, and brought him presents. Though he was grateful to them, he nursed a restless and seething anger that defied rational explanation and he reacted badly to whatever the nuns did. He rebelled against them for no just reason and began to steal from the donation box. Then he pilfered a silver chalice and antique brass candlesticks, sold them to a fence and used the money to buy marijuana. He bore the Sisters no malice. They were his only family, and a loving family, but he couldn't control his own actions.

One late afternoon, while the nuns were visiting a hospital in another city, Osmond sold a merchant all the pews, chairs and kneeling benches in the church. They closed the deal with wine from the sacristy. He relished the shocked expression on the Mother Superior's face when the sisters returned the next day. He went to his room and laughed until his sides ached. When she asked her little darling what happened, he told her. The nuns went to the merchant's shop and demanded that he return his purchases.

The merchant had already sold most of the pews and kneeling benches to another church in Brooklyn. After days of pleading, cursing and praying, the nuns retrieved the furniture and Osmond was punished severely. The School Board warned him that the next prank would lead to expulsion, and possibly reform school.

His need to create havoc and to annoy those gentle creatures was beyond rational understanding. Time and again they offered to get him help, but he always refused. He made friends with local prostitutes and invited them into the church school. They enjoyed having sex with a midget in a nunnery. One evening, while the nuns were at vespers, the girls and Osmond had a party. They drank and caroused in his small room until the noise disturbed the sisters. The Mother Superior left the chapel and found Osmond in bed with four prostitutes. He invited her to join them. The expression of horror on her face was more than he could handle. While the girls dressed and fled, Osmond laughed until his sides ached. In tears, the Mother Superior called the police and recommended that he be sent to a reform school.

The idea didn't appeal to Osmond. He packed a few things, slipped out of the building through a side door, and never saw the nuns again.

"I didn't weigh the effects of my pranks," Osmond said to me. "I loved darkness, the mystery of evil, playing the anti–hero and pretending that I was the one flaw in a perfect tapestry."

Not interested in money or pleasure or the immediate rewards of his activities, he enjoyed upsetting the balance, and rebelling against any dogma imposed upon him. He would most likely have brought virtue to a whorehouse. In fact, he spent hours lecturing the ladies of the night on ways and means of changing their ways.

He slept in flophouses and on subway gratings, in alleyways and hallways, until one evening, fed up with being hungry and always on the run he went to the roof of a tenement building on Bryant Avenue. He had finished off a pint of vodka, and his head was unclear. The building seemed to be moving and he stared aimlessly at a starry sky. Then he looked down from the rooftop at the streets as if into a bottomless pit.

It's simple enough, he thought. Just hurl yourself to the pavement. In one moment it will be over. A crowd will gather, and after a little confusion, they'll take the body away. The men at the morgue will have autopsy practice, and life will go on as usual.

The pavement below became his mortal enemy.

"All I wanted to do was feel some connection to another person," he said to me, "to speak with someone, to touch him or her, and to know what it's like to love another human being. There's nothing worse than being alone in the world, and no greater pain than the pain of isolation."

While he gazed frantically into the black hole beneath him and tried to muster the courage to jump, he heard, in the distance, the sound of a flute. "It's my own mad mind conjuring up illusions," he said to himself. But when he turned his head in the direction of the music, he saw a legless man riding on a dolly that was pushed by four children. He played a haunting melody on his flute; and the sound of his sweet music filled the empty city streets. Behind him were dozens of boys and girls singing and dancing and having a good time.

"The dreamlike procession passed beneath me and made its way up a hill on the next block where an audience had gathered to watch The Dancing Man," Osmond said to me. "My eyes were glued to the legless man."

But the flute player disappeared in the assemblage of people gathered to watch The Dancing Man perform; and Osmond, who couldn't take his eyes off the masked specter, no longer considered suicide. He left the rooftop, walked up the Bryant Avenue hill and joined the audience. The rest was simple: he returned to the hill night after night and joined the convocation of people that had gathered there to take in the show; and one evening, Rachel invited him to follow her into the door of the burned–out building.

"I have been here ever since," Osmond said laughing, "helping The Elder and serving The Dancing Man. But, trust me, Joshua when I tell you that I don't worship him. He's my teacher, that's all, and someday I hope to fully ingest the wisdom he imparts to those who are in his circle."

"And the flute player?" I asked.

"Never saw him again. I've looked for him, and I've asked around the neighborhood, but no one seems to know who he is. It's all very strange to me, but no stranger than living in an orphanage and on the streets." There was a twinkle in his eye and a sense of well-being about him. He had found his home and was grateful to The Dancing Man. "Come," he said to me. "The Elder is waiting for you."

A very young boy sat next to the entrance to The Elder's chambers. He was skinny and pale and looked at us with perplexity. Next to him stood an old man in a worn tuxedo and a high black hat. He resembled an uncle of mine who had died many years ago.

Osmond gave the old man a coin as we passed.

"God be with you," said the old man, tipping his hat. He grabbed my arm. "My grandson is waiting to see The Dancing Man." His grip was surprisingly strong for a person of his age. "It takes a long time," he continued. "Do you have a moment? Please sit with us."

"Leave him alone!" Osmond commanded.

"It's all right," I said. The old man made a place for me and I sat down with him and his grandson. Osmond glared, but didn't say anything.

"I was summoned by The Elder a month ago," the old man said in a hushed voice. "Osmond escorted me here, but he never explained why. 'What do you have to know?' he asked me. 'Come along. You'll find out the reasons later.' I went with him, but was afraid. I did not know what they wanted from me...if anything. I began to think they called me here to just to have me sit and wait.

"I've committed no crime!" he shouted at me. "Tom here was always with me.

"Why have they brought me here? I've done no harm to anyone. They've never explained anything to me. All I get are stares, and I watch them whisper among themselves. I haven't, as yet, gotten one explanation. But their looks, their silent appraisals of Tom and me speak loudly that we're guilty of something. What can it be, my friend? Why do they persist? Why do they torment me?

"I'm a simple man...a lonely man. All I have is Tom, and I'm sure they're gonna take him away from me. They pulled me out of bed and dragged me here. Why, I ask you, what am I guilty of? I don't trust them. They want to steal my person, my individuality and my grandson.

"You've got to listen to me, young man. You know why? I'll tell you, but first take a good look. Who am I?"

"I don't know," I replied.

"I'm your uncle, you fool," the old man said. He laughed wildly. The child also laughed. "I'm your uncle in this dream."

I pushed him away, but he tightened his grip on my arm.

"No, wait," he said. "There's something you don't know. The Elder's a decent sort. He used to own the delicatessen on 173rd Street, but now he's in cahoots with The Dancing Man. You'll probably remember him. 'There's nothing to fear,' The Elder once said to me. I drew back from him. 'I promise,' he went on, 'if you just listen to me.' I looked directly into his eyes and said, 'I wonder if a man can live in this world without being accused of a crime.' 'I am not accusing you,' he replied. 'Where is The Dancing Man?' I demanded. There was no answer. 'Where is he?' I repeated again.

"'He's not available,' The Elder said to me. 'Why?' I shouted at him and told him emphatically that I don't deal with underlings. The Elder sighed and told Osmond to take me home. 'They don't know who I am,' I said to Tom. 'They think I'm mad. But a madman would never question them.'"

The old man let go of my arm, stood up, and said, "Me and Tom, we have our dreams. You bet your life that we do, and no dancing fool's gonna mess with them. You'll never guess what I asked The Elder."

"What?" I responded, happy to no longer be in the clutches of this mad old person.

"I asked him if he'd ever ridden on the wings of a swan. 'No,' he replied. Then I asked him if he'd ever touched the tentacles of a spider that dangled from the moon? 'No,' he replied. He just stood there and looked at me, shook his head and whispered to Oswald that I'm nuts. 'You're all like me,' I told him. 'You're all dreamers, and the worst dreamer of all is The Dancing Man. He's Death itself, that one. He needs to find something more important to busy himself with, something to keep him from meddling in human affairs.'

"'Get him out of here,' The Elder said to Osmond.

"'How did the owner of a delicatessen get into such a position of power?' I asked him. "'Whom did you sleep with?'

"'Now, right now, take him somewhere else,' he said angrily to Oswald.

"'*There are ten thousand swans,'* I sang in a soft voice, *'flying through the clouds.*

"'You will not take them away from me...nor Tom....poor Tom...his mother and father are dead.'

"I begged them not to rob us of our dreams. 'You know something,' I said to Oswald, 'I have been to a mountaintop, I've talked with the wind, I've seen The Dancing Man dance his dance of death.'

"They took me home. They took your uncle home. But home was a lonely place. All Tom did was sit and cry. I made him some soup, but he didn't want any. What's a kid to do? His mother and father are dead. He's stuck with an old fart like me and I feel as if I'm floating on threads of cloud that pass over the city. There's no corner to crawl into and the Elder thinks I'm the last of the mad ones." He picked up his grandson and took him in his arms. "Tom understands me," the old man said. "We're pals no matter what happens." The child nestled in the old man's arms. "Perhaps I am mad," he went on. "If so, The Elder in his wisdom is judging the actions of a mad person. He in his profound wisdom..."

He broke off and began to sob.

"The birds will fly above the building," he went on, "and they don't give a damn about The Elder or The Dancing Man. They do not sit and wait."

"Is there anything I can do, old man?" I asked him.

"No," he smiled. "But thank you. The birds will fly whether the rains come or not — and I'll always be a fool. But I have Tom. If you think about it, what else do I need?"

Osmond and I walked away.

"You can take everything from a man but his dreams," said Osmond. "He hopes that the future will bring a better life. I don't know if it's a useful hope or the height of absurdity."

"Some of us learn," I ventured.

"Yes, but very few," he responded.

When Osmond was first brought to the burned-out building, he also asked The Elder what kind of a crime he had committed. Osmond told him that the old man had his swans and he had an ark.

"Haven't all the great men of history navigated one kind of an ark or another?" he railed. "Leonardo piloted an ark. So did Michelangelo, Shakespeare, Mozart, Galileo, and Thomas Jefferson. History calls them inspired, but they, too, were judged by an Elder, and had to defend their right to exist. They believed in themselves and took a chance. If they hadn't, there would be no history. I'd prefer to be a member of their legion even if I'm accused of being a madman and a dreamer."

He was so obsessed with himself that he didn't recognize the wisdom in The Elder.

"Nobody has accused you of anything," The Elder replied. "All these geniuses!" he shrugged his shoulders. "Even if you are on their side, they don't believe you. They rebel against anything that moves. Genius without maturity is a dangerous thing."

Osmond refused to accept The Elder as a friend.

"He was nothing more to me than a bureaucrat sitting on a dais," Osmond said, "and in my mind, we were natural enemies. When I look back, Joshua, I see how foolish I was, telling him that Little Jack Osmond couldn't be made to hide from his dreams."

The Elder had told Osmond that he would help him build the ark; that he would also help him navigate any dangerous waters, but first, Osmond had to trust The Dancing Man.

"There's always a condition," Osmond replied. "What if I can't?"

"Then I can do nothing for you," The Elder said. "You might as well return to the roof and meditate on the sidewalk below."

"But how can I trust him if I don't trust myself? I'm an orphan. I have no roots, no family. I'm always looking up to some elder to tell me how to run my life. If someone would just tell me where I can find my home."

"This is home." The Elder said.

Two years ago, Osmond's home was an orphanage; then it was the streets; then he thought it would be an asylum; and only a month ago he was going to kill himself.

"Now I'm here," Osmond said to The Elder, "and Jack's-a-dancin' round his imaginary ark — he's-a-sailin' to the moon; poor, poor Jack's-a-sailin' to the moon." The Elder put his arm around Osmond's shoulder. "I've never trusted anyone," Osmond said to him. "Not even the nuns at the orphanage."

"It's time to begin," The Elder replied.

"'But how?'

"Work for The Dancing Man; have patience and try to love yourself. You're worthy of sailing around the moon. You just have to learn how to navigate the ark."

"He'll teach me that?"

"Yes."

"Then let's begin."

Osmond shook The Elder's hand and accepted the burned-out building as his home, and, ever since, he's worked steadily for The Dancing Man.

The Elder's chamber was a large room with oak paneling and Victorian pews and railings around a dais on which he sat. There were eight-to-ten feet high gothic windows that overlooked a garden, and birds fluttered outside. Many clerks scurried here and there, and a gallery of men, women and children watched us from a slightly raised balcony in the rear. These people were shadow-like, but their faces were familiar to me. They were friends and relatives come here to plead their case with The Elder. Other clerks, seemingly more important, sat on stools at high pedestal desks, and their elongated shadows looked like they were painted onto the floor.

The Elder had a stern expression on his face and continued to look at me until his stare became uncomfortable. It was funny to think that I knew this man from the old neighborhood. He was a good friend of my father's and once ran a delicatessen.

"Mr. Lewis!" I said. "I didn't know you lived here."

"Yes," he replied, his face softened, and he no longer stared at me.

"My father told me that you had moved." I said nervously. "Did you know he's dying?"

"Yes. I visited him about a week ago."

"He didn't tell me," I replied. "But you? How did you get here?"

"I'm not sure, Joshua, how I got into your dream. What's amazing is that I've become your creation. Do you remember the talks we used to have when you were just a kid?"

"Yes."

"I enjoyed them, but always knew that things would change. It was a sad day for me when you went away to college, and now your father's dying." He took a deep breath and said to me, "I've been told that The Dancing Man sees promise in you."

"Promise?"

"As his protégée."

"Protégée? What the hell is that? My father's in the hospital and may not live out the night, and I came here to watch The Dancing Man like I did when I was a child. I just wanted to relive a few happy moments from my life. What's really strange is that I seem to be getting lost in this dream."

"You can wake up."

"How?"

He looked at me for a long time, shrugged his shoulders, and said, "I don't know."

"I'm not guilty of my father's death," I said. My voice cracked and I couldn't look him in the face.

"No one has blamed you," he responded.

"Then why am I here?" I asked with a trembling voice. "Why am I in your chamber — your courtroom!"

"Because you want to be."

"Then it's not a dream?"

"That's not what I said. Do you know how many people come through this room? They all have one problem or another. In the last five years, I've listened to every conceivable excuse for success and failure. There are no new ones, yet each person thinks his condition is unique. Each person marvels at the nightmarish creatures that live in his mind and he believes that his madness is finer than his fellow man's.

"If we could only stand back and look at our lives," he continued talking. His eyes were like two burning coals that penetrated the core of my being. He certainly wasn't the Mr. Lewis I remembered from the old neighborhood. "We would be horrified at the energy we pour into matters of no consequence. We would see that the guilt we feel comes from our inability to accept our worth as human beings. Does it matter if we do something wrong? Will anyone remember an hour later? People are too busy worrying about other people's mistakes to pay much attention to their own, and yet, if you think about it, the punishment we inflict on ourselves is much more severe than the punishment dealt us by the outer world.

"So why do anything?" he asked rhetorically. "The answer is simple. We need and want certain things — like money, or love or success — and we must work to attain them; and each step on the ladder that leads to these goals gives deeper insight into our self and what obstacles we put in our own way."

Mr. Lewis had lived in the neighborhood for most of his life, and had become old and a little tired, as if five years of answering people's questions had worn him down. He grew up here, married here, and his daughter was born here.

He put his hand on my shoulder and said softly, "I remember you as a child, Joshua, playing in the streets."

He would leave his deli in the afternoons and watch my friends and I shoot baskets in the P.S. 50 schoolyard or chase one another around parked cars and through back alleyways.

"Do you remember when you boys set fire to the old house by the river? What a commotion that caused," he laughed, "but you were kids and trouble came naturally. I never paid it much attention, because I knew that you and your friends would grow out of it one day."

He sat down in an armchair next to his desk and looked at me with a pleasant smile on his face. He and my father used to go to a local bar on Boston Road, order a couple of beers and talk for hours. When my father introduced him to my mother, he so wanted Mr. Lewis to like her. He asked her to dress up and took them both out to a fancy restaurant.

"Your dad and I had some swell times together," The Elder said to me in a sad voice. "I'm going to miss him."

Though he had known about The Dancing Man from his early childhood, it never occurred to Mr. Lewis to go to see him.

"When life is good to us," The Elder said, "we assume it will last forever. I was a simple man, Joshua. I had no dream of sailing on an ark, like Osmond. In fact, I still think he's a little mad."

"Mad or a poet," I said.

The Elder looked pensive, and I could sense a deep sorrow in him.

He had worked fourteen hours a day to support his family. They were everything to him and they loved one another very much. He had a few plans, not big ones mind you, but plans nonetheless: someday a house in the country...college for his girl. He and his wife spoke about these plans almost every day until he came home one evening and found his apartment in shambles. His wife and daughter both lay dead on the floor. They had been beaten, raped, and left to die in a pool of their own blood. That scene engraved itself in his memory.

"I remember it well, Mr. Lewis," I said to him.

"Talk about fantasy and vision, Joshua. Can any dream compare with that reality?

He left his apartment in a state of shock and walked up the hill to where The Dancing Man was performing, leaned against a building and watched him move like a specter in the wind. For some unknown reason, he returned every night for many months. The dance was like a drug that absorbed his mind and psyche and made him forget — at least temporarily — the horror of his wife and daughter's deaths. One day, about five years ago, he was asked to assume the role of Elder.

"Believe it or not, Joshua, my pain hasn't diminished," he said. "But I listen and I learn from everyone who comes before my bench, and being The Elder has kept me from killing myself."

There was something of the old Mr. Lewis about him — that kind man who always had time to talk to me — that compassionate soul who never refused giving a cup of coffee to someone on the bum.

"A few weeks ago," The Elder said, "Norman Dawes, a kid from the neighborhood, now in his early twenties, showed up here. He had just been released from a Spanish prison. He was an artist and he wanted his prison experience to help him explore through art deeper realms of human consciousness. He told me stories about his life in jail."

There was a young Arabic man named Mohammet in the cell near him. He, and two of his friends had rowed a boat from Morocco across the Straits of Gibraltar to Spain. After several days, and totally exhausted, they landed on a beach that was part of a Spanish army base. Surrounded by soldiers with rifles and machine guns, they were arrested as spies.

The early evenings were filled with the screams of Mohammet being raped by guards. One morning, in the yard, he told Dawes that he would either kill himself or his principle tormentor, and when the guard came to his cell and ordered him to undress that evening, Mohammet sat down on the floor.

"If you want me," he said, "you will have to kill me first. I'm sick of your game, and I've got nothing to live for. Come on! Kill me!"

At first the guard laughed and struck Mohammet in the face.

"Come on!" he taunted the guard. "I want to die. Let's see how quickly you can kill me. You've had your fun. Now it's time to kill the kitty."

The guard called two or three others. They talked it over, and left. It was as if Mohammet had offended them. They could rape him, but they were afraid to kill him.

"There's a point at which the indignities of the world are more than we can bear," the artist said to The Elder, "and Mohammet's was a victory of sorts. He was alive and the guards left him alone. A few weeks later he was tried. I never heard from him again."

In the cell next to Dawes, there was an English inmate who was a pawn in a political struggle — something he thought that had to do with Gibraltar. The Englishman had a terrible disease of the liver.

"I'd lay awake at night and listen to his screams until I started shaking in my own bed," Dawes said. "I cursed the guards and the warden and turned on the Englishman himself. They finally came and took him away, then unlocked my cell, stared at me, and laughed. I was released shortly thereafter."

The streets of Malaga took on a different sheen now that Dawes saw them with the eyes of a free man. The Spanish architecture with iron-gated windows and balustrades on Merced Square and Larios Street had that quaint sense of the antique that made him realize how many thousands of people — all of them with ideas, dreams and visions — had walked these streets before he ever knew they existed. He ordered a meal in an outdoor restaurant and delighted in the wine, the fish, the vegetables, and in the people sitting around him. The trees shimmered in a noonday sun that reflected from windows across the street, and he discovered minor miracles that happened to him each day: a cup of fresh ground coffee, *tapas*, a glass of wine, just walking down the street, wandering by himself on the beach. Stoned on life and free of the prison, he thought the buzz would never end. But weeks passed, and he began to take for granted the very things he once thought were miracles. Trapped in a self-made prison — more like a stink hole full of negative thoughts — he decided to visit The Dancing Man. He had lost sight of even the simplest things.

The Elder poured some coffee and said to me thoughtfully, "Norman stayed here for a few months and left. It's funny, Joshua, but basic human needs never change. No two people are alike and that's one of life's great miracles. We must learn to respect each person's individuality. We are not born to tear one another to pieces.

"For my part," The Elder went on, "each day, I crawl up a very steep craggy mountain an inch at a time. If I don't watch my step, I might kill a grasshopper or a beetle. Some say it doesn't matter, but I prefer to respect the earth and all its creatures."

"What is at the top of the mountain?" I asked him.

"I don't know, and I don't even know if it matters," The Elder replied. "Perhaps there's nothing; perhaps just another mountain to climb, and another. Why must there always be a treasure at the end of our struggles? Wouldn't it be wonderful to climb to the summit and discover an empty sky? We live with expectations, and we defeat ourselves when the ends are not what we imagined they'd be. What if we expected nothing? If we accepted our gifts as they came? Imagine the joy we would take in what we found along the way."

The Elder nodded his head in the direction of a large restless group of supplicants in the gallery that were all there to get his advice. "Let's talk later," he said to me. "I've got to attend to them."

On leaving The Elder's chamber, my first thought was to find an exit to the street, but, no matter how thoroughly I explored the building, I found nothing more than labyrinthine corridors in a dark maze of windowless rooms.

"I've got to return to the hospital," I said to myself. "I've got to see my father, speak with him, and get his blessing before he dies."

"Don't worry about me, Joshua." It was my father's voice. "These last moments are the best."

"Where are you?" I cried out.

"In your thoughts, my son, in your dreams, in a place where I'll always be."

"But I must see you."

"You will, I promise, but never as you saw me before."

I continued to walk, but my legs grew weak and my head spun like a carousel that ran amok. Lights flashed on and off, and I could hear cars in the distance, but there didn't seem to be any exit from the building.

Tired and disorientated, my legs buckled from beneath me. I fell to the floor and lay there for what seemed like an eternity. My knees were curled against my chest and when I finally got up, I noticed an open window permitting sunlight to flood one corner of the room. Rachel was sitting at a desk busy doing paperwork. A faint light shone on her face.

There was a timeless and primitive quality to her beauty. With high cheekbones, oval brown eyes and long black hair, a well-shaped chin, and soft, but curvaceous lips, she had won the hearts of most of the young men in my high school, and was voted most popular in her senior year. We dated for two years, and split after graduation when I decided to attend a college out of town.

"Good morning," she said, "or should I say good afternoon. I thought you were going to sleep forever."

"Am I still in the burned-out building?" I asked her.

"Yes," she smiled."

"Then it's still a dream."

"Unless things have changed," she replied and began to shuffle some papers.

"I heard my father's voice," I said to her. "But I can't get to him. He's dying, Rachel, and this goddamn dream has consumed me."

"Yes, I know."

"It's been many years since we two were together," I said to her.

"At least four," she replied.

"Now you're here."

"Yes," she said. "I help The Dancing Man."

"Like Osmond and The Elder?" I asked. "Are you also learning his ways?"

"I'm trying, Joshua. But it takes so long. Sometimes I feel as if I'm walking up a hundred-flight stairwell ass-backwards."

"I've thought about you a lot," I said.

"I have a child, now."

"I know. My mother wrote me."

"We share a room at the end of the building. She's three years-old."

Rachel had changed little over the last four years. The same lightness in her voice and dark eyes that seemed so deep and ancient, yet remain untouched and retained an innocence that opened deep into her soul.

"Do you remember the summer evenings, Joshua, when we watched him dance?"

"But this is different. There was no mystery then. There were no Osmonds or Elders, and we sat together and laughed like children. We enjoyed the music and his dance."

"A great deal can change in four years."

"I know, Rachel. My father is dying, and you have a child. I must see him again, if only for a moment before he passes over."

"Then wake up."

"I can't. It's as if The Dancing Man has taken control of all my senses. I have the feeling that he has a great secret to tell me."

"He does."

"But why does it take so long? I don't even know where he is."

"He'll be on the street at seven o'clock. You can see him then."

"And meanwhile?"

"You could meet my daughter." She looked at me and smiled. "I'm crazy about her, Joshua. I love it when she nestles against me and nibbles at my fingers and laughs so freely when I kiss her on the stomach or when I pretend to take a big bite out of her behind; I loved it when her lips touched my nipples and my milk flowed into her. There are no conditions in our relationship. Can you imagine? She lived inside me. I was no more than a vehicle for her birth. If you want an instant education in selflessness, then raise a child. She cries at three or four o'clock in the morning without regard to time or place; she's either hungry or has wet her bed or is scared; and it doesn't matter how tired you are. You still have to find that extra bit of energy. There's no use complaining, because she won't listen. Her only way of reaching you is by crying, and it is never without a reason. Sometimes she wants to be held, or fed. Sometimes I talk to her, or sing her a song. If you love someone, it transforms you into a minor league martyr. There isn't much time for yourself."

"And her father?" I asked.

"He left me when he found out that I was pregnant."

"Sounds like a shit to me," I said.

"No, not really," she replied. "A little bit of a pain in the ass, but not a shit. I mean, he wanted me to have an abortion, and, at first, I considered it, but decided to have the baby. He was just a kid, Joshua, and couldn't bear the responsibility of having a real child. He told me that it would interfere with his plans and I watched, sometimes with horror, his self-assured facade vanish with my pregnancy. I wasn't angry. I just wanted him to leave. I saw his true nature, and it was easier for me to deal with the situation alone."

She began to play with the buttons on my shirt. "It's been a long time," she said. I kissed her on the lips and stroked her hair. I ran my fingers over the contour of her body, cupping her breasts and touching her thighs lightly.

"We were once two kids playing at love," I said to her with a smile, "and the fantasies were more pleasant than the awkward realities."

"Do you think it's any different now?" she asked. She took off my shirt and unbuckled my trousers. "It takes time to learn to make love to another human being. Once we played at it; now we might take it too seriously."

We undressed and lay together on the cot, Rachel nestled in my arms and her lips pressed gently against my neck. I touched her face and ran my fingers over her forehead, cheeks, nose and stomach, and along the line of her neck to a point between her breasts.

"I love you, Joshua." Her soft and heartfelt voice made the dream-like world of The Dancing Man seem safe. After we made love, I closed my eyes and saw my father's image floating in the darkness.

"I know very well what it is to be a prisoner of life," he said.

"What do you mean?" I asked him.

"I hid from it, Joshua. You know how difficult it was for me to love anyone. But death and dying has shown me another path."

I opened my eyes and Rachel was sitting next to me.

"You were so restless," she said. I reached out and took her hand, and tried to collect my thoughts.

"If there's anything to learn in this strange world, it's got to be the art of being in love," I said to her.

"I've got to go," she replied. "The Dancing Man sent a messenger and asked me to come to his chambers. We'll see each other later."

"It's always later," I said to her, "but at least we'll see each other; at least I can hold you in my arms and make love to you."

"Anything's possible in Joshua's dream," she laughed, "and The Dancing Man's world."

⁂

The late afternoon sun filtered through the window and painted dark shadows on the floor and walls of the room. From the window, I saw well-trimmed gardens that led down to a river. Men and women strolled together and children played assorted games on the grass. Some of the passersby looked up and waved to me.

The sunlight's odd brightness had an otherworldly effect — an ethereal, almost Day-Glo vision of light clinging to every person on the lawn — a peaceable kingdom of sorts, where monkeys swung from trees and lions and tigers walked with deer and moose, and children played games of tag and hide-and-seek. The Dancing Man sat near the river quietly perusing the scene. He was dressed in a black, tight-fitting outfit with a white mask. Rachel was next to him. He nodded at me. I returned his greeting, and decided to join him in the garden. But, to my surprise, and chagrin, the door to my room led directly into Elder's chambers; and he was busily quieting a crowd of sick, deformed, deaf, blind and scabrous supplicants that wanted to see the Dancing Man. There were women and children, old men and young couples, all with pitiable looks on their faces — some chanting, others praying and others screaming, and the nonstop cacophony drowned any thought I had of going down to the garden and spending time with Rachel and The Dancing Man. The front door to his chamber burst open and an army of beggars pressed their way into the overcrowded room and created even more of a commotion. The din grew so loud that it was almost impossible to make out The Elder's voice.

"Why won't The Dancing Man see these people?" I asked Osmond, who stood next to me. "He's not busy. I just saw him sitting in the garden."

"What can he do, Joshua? He dances every evening and asks them for nothing. If we let them through, they'll tear him apart. The Dancing Man isn't going to save the world by himself. He plants seeds of self-knowledge and time does the rest. It takes years of work to master his art, and you, my dear friend, have the opportunity to learn how. Please. I'm begging you to take advantage of it — for your sake, for mine, for everyone in this room. Overcome your fear and ask of life for nothing but the strength to serve a Higher Principle. If The Dancing Man were to vanish from the world, what would these people do? His presence gives them hope. I mean, who can live without hope...

"When I first came here," he said with tears in his eyes, "a few supplicants were before the bench. Now there are hundreds, and soon, thousands will come. The suffering and despair of people seems to get more intense every day. Sometimes I dislike him when he dances. I mean his detachment drives me crazy. But, he is always there. Time passes, the crowds change, and he continues to dance." Then Osmond took my hand and said, "Love him, Joshua. He is your real father."

I stepped out of The Elder's chamber and entered a main hall in which thirty-foot high walls were covered with faded mosaic tiles depicting battle scenes. Dark curtains covered the windows. Many office doors were open off its vestibule and the sound of clerical activities echoed throughout, and I could see assorted typists and clerks, and a few stalwart–looking gents dressed in pinstriped suits, who must have been executives of some sort. They were all middle–aged, pale and drawn, and the workers' heads were elongated apparitions attached to tiny bodies. None of them spoke as much as they barked, and it sounded as if every sentence was a command. These vigilant, almost specter–like people performed routine tasks with determination. But no one looked up or even noticed me, and I left them to their work. It was imperative for me to speak with The Dancing Man, and I believed that I could approach him directly. When I parted a window's curtain and looked outside, I expected to see The Dancing Man presiding over his peaceable kingdom. Instead, there were rows of brick tenements and fenced–in back alleys with clotheslines strung from window to window.

The door to The Elder's chamber opened and emitted a clamor that filled the hallway.

Why is he so difficult to get to? I thought. Every evening at 7:00 he dances on the street and crowds of people watch him. He would probably dance if the streets were empty...

"You're still trying to understand, aren't you?" It was Rachel. She put her arm through mine and rested her head on my shoulder.

"Marthe's my miracle child," she said in a soft, but clear voice," and she's taught me so much from the first moment of her life."

The very act of giving birth to Marthe had transformed Rachel. She had finally learned the meaning of unconditional love. "I was just a vehicle through which another human being came into the world," she said to me, "and Marthe turned every negative sensation in me into a life–giving energy."

At first, Marthe asked for so little — some caring, food and warmth, simple things, and in return, a river of love poured out of her. Rachel bathed in it; she rejoiced in it, but after a few months, she began to resent Marthe's presence. Rachel was always tired and irritable, and baby Marthe cried, was hungry, and needed attention.

"I couldn't go out," she said to Joshua. "If I wanted to be with a man, I had to consider Marthe. If I stepped into the other room, she began to cry. She became more of an imposition than a love child — a trespasser on all my time and space."

One night, Marthe's crying became relentless, and she refused to stop. Her voice grated on Rachel (who hadn't slept for days), and sent shivers through every part of her body. "I hated her, Joshua, and it scared me, but I've got to tell you the truth — I could have killed her on the spot. In exasperation, I broke down and cried like a baby. It was everything I could do to keep from hitting her. I was alone and incapable of loving her — with no one to talk to. It frightened me to think that I might hurt my own child."

After ten frightful minutes filled with tension, Rachel finally relaxed, and nestled Marthe in her arms.

"'My child,' I said, 'my little baby. Please don't cry.'"

All Rachel wanted was to love her child, and be responsible for her. She just didn't know how. That evening, she went to see The Dancing Man. The Elder invited her into the building and they went to his chamber.

"I wanted to kill my daughter," she said to him, "but I love her, and more than anything else, I want to take care of her. I just don't have the strength. How could things change so quickly? Sometimes I'm afraid to even look in the mirror."

The Elder put his arms around Rachel. He told her that there are no vacations when you have a child. There are no places to hide. You quickly learn that lip service love has little or no value when it comes to raising her.

"Marthe is as much a part of you as your own heart," he said with a smile. "There's no escaping her. The love she has for her mother will follow no matter where you attempt to hide. Stop complaining about your life, stop living like an emotionally crippled seven year–old in an adult's body. You've taken motherhood upon yourself, so be kind to yourself and learn that a mother must love her child unconditionally."

The Elder sat in his chair. He had a world–weary smile on his face and looked at Rachel with soft eyes so full of love that she had never experienced anything like it before.

"'It is easy to bring Marthe up according to your own ideas,' he said, 'but she's unique, and she is not you. You have to trust her, and you have to learn, as well, to trust yourself. She will find her own path. Someday you will die, and you don't want her to die with you. She is not your creation, and the problems you will confront together will force both of you to become more human. You must respect her life, and understand that you did not conceive her in order to keep her from living it."

Rachel stopped talking for a moment, looked at me, smiled and said, "Can you imagine being angry at Marthe? Can you believe that I felt like killing her? I shudder to think how angry and resentful I was. She was an innocent, helpless infant and I might have hurt her."

She lifted my hand to her lips and kissed it. Then we sat in silence for a long time before she resumed talking.

"About six months ago, I went to Portugal with Marthe."

They had spent time in a small fishing village called Lagos in the Algarve. Every evening they'd sit on the beach and watch the shadows shift on the sand. There were fishermen weaving nets and repairing boats, and one or two people strolled near the water. Rachel had nothing to do but watch the subtle changes of light and darkness fall on the beach. The ocean breeze cut through the warm summer air and a group of men played cards near the shore. Shadow–like and in dark shirts, they huddled over a table. They spoke in Portuguese and from time to time, one or all of them would burst into laughter. Rachel couldn't make out one word they said to each other, but it didn't matter to her. She had created her own version of their conversation, and she thought this had to be better than the mundane exchange of words that goes on in most people's lives. These men became whatever she wanted them to be.

"The sky darkened," she said to me. "I got drowsy, checked on Marthe, and I was happy to see her sleeping. A delightful breeze came off the ocean and relaxed every part of my body. The drowsiness spread and I also fell into a light sleep."

The dark figures of the card players dominated her thoughts, and their slow, deliberate movements drew her further into a dream. About a hundred feet from the water's edge, she saw a large oil slick forcing countless dead fish to wash ashore and come to rest at the card players' feet. These dead fish sparkled in the moon's light, and in no way interfered with the ongoing card game. When she awoke, the card players were gone and the moonlit night revealed a constant beating of white breakers against the beach. There was no oil slick. She gathered Marthe in her arms and they returned to their hotel room.

"Every evening, when Marthe and I sat on the beach, the card players were there. They'd nod and wave to us, but I never spoke to them. I didn't want to ruin the quaint picture I had made in my mind of a place so peaceful I thought I would never experience its likes again; I didn't want to taint that picture with chitchat about mundane things."

The Elder always spoke about a bridge we have to cross that connects our personal ideas of life with the rest of the world. He told Rachel that we're all human and we need to communicate our needs to one another

— we all want to love and be loved.

"I haven't crossed that bridge, as yet, but, Joshua dear," she said and kissed me on the cheek, "for the first time in my life, I have the courage to do it."

The evening before they left Lagos, Marthe and Rachel went to the beach and discovered that the card players were gone. Marthe wanted to know where the men were. 'I don't know,' Rachel told her. 'Then let's go,' Marthe said. 'I want to play with my doll.'

"It's hard to imagine Marthe losing her simple grace," Rachel said to me, "but it will happen, my God it will really happen. Like every other child, she'll get older. That simple grace will disappear, and she'll have to seek out The Dancing Man and find her way back to a state of innocence.

"Marthe and my father would make a remarkable pair," I said. "She with her innocence and he with his wisdom. The last time I saw him, he had a childlike expression on his face. His eyes twinkled like Marthe's eyes twinkle and I could look in them and see an open heart."

"They'd be good friends," Rachel laughed and kissed me again. "In almost every way, Marthe's my teacher," she continued. "I watch her explore the world."

Then Rachel told me that Marthe could create a magic kingdom from wooden sticks or paper matches or sipping straws. She talks to imaginary friends, make–believe pets, and nature spirits. Give her a crayon and she'll produce a masterpiece, but not just on paper — on floors, walls, tables — on anything with a flat surface. Her world has no boundaries. Everything is a mystery and needs to be explored.

"Just think, Joshua, if all the things we take for granted were unfamiliar to us, if we experienced them for the first time: eating with a fork, flushing the toilet, getting into bed, clothing ourselves, and so on. All of life would be an adventure. We would never be bored.

"The Elder once told me that great mysteries are hidden in mundane things. 'The idea and the experience of the idea,' The Elder said, 'are separated by a chasm filled with fears and doubts. To travel from one to the other is a voyage only the most daring or innocent will take.'

"Come with me," she said. "We're going to see him now. He has some time and promised to tell me about Tobias Hume, The Dancing Man's teacher."

She opened a door in the main room, and we entered The Elder's chambers. There wasn't a supplicant or penitent to be seen, and The Elder sat in an armchair near the window.

"Have a seat," The Elder said. "I will tell you what I know about Tobias Hume."

"Where are all the people?" I asked him.

"I don't know," he replied. "They might be at lunch or dinner or whatever they do this time of day. I have a little time, so let's not waste it."

"I've always wanted to know about Tobias Hume," Rachel said.

"Yes," The Elder answered. "An interesting person who trained The Dancing Man."

Then he proceeded to tell the following story:

When Hume was in his mid-forties, he set out to find Thule, an octogenarian who lived on an island off the Florida coast. The island lay in the middle of a channel in which currents and reefs played havoc with the boats that approached. He had heard about an ancient legend that concerned a gift of prophecy that was handed down from generation to generation. It was said that Thule was the possessor of this secret. He was an irascible old man who preferred his solitude to the society of other men and was notorious for turning visitors away. Hume set out in a sailboat and navigated the channel to within a few miles of the island. Strong breakers and rocks that jutted out of the water wrecked his boat, and Hume had to swim the rest of the way to shore. Thule found him half-dead on the beach, and gruffly asked what right he had to trespass.

"I've come to see Thule," Hume answered weakly.

"He's gone away. He won't be back for six months."

"Does he take students?"

"He gave up teaching twenty years ago. Couldn't find anyone who would listen. He's sent some thirty-odd people away this year. Told them to spend the next decade listening to bird calls and street sounds; told them that they must become practiced listeners."

"My boat hit a reef.

"I'll give you a dinghy. You can row back to the mainland and try again in six months. But I guarantee nothing. He's as slippery as they get and there's no telling what he'll do or say."

Hume made the trip to the island many times and the old man sent him away, always with another excuse. Finally, Hume simply refused to leave. He threatened to build a cabin on the beach and wait for Thule.

"Build whatever the hell you want," the old man said. "Maybe you'll be lucky and by the time you're finished, Thule will find it in his grisly heart to see you."

Hume worked on the cabin for seven months. He had to cut and fit each log by hand; he put in windows and floors, and framed the doorways. In all that time, he never saw the old man or Thule. One morning, as he sat on a bench admiring his completed cabin, the old man stepped out of the forest.

"It takes seven years," he said, "from the moment you start studying with a master for his teachings to take root."

"You're Thule!" Hume said with astonishment, but the old man didn't answer.

"A disciple who leaves any time before the seven years are up will lose all understanding of what he was taught," the old man said.

Hume laughed until he wept and the old man laughed with him. Soon they both lay in the sand exhausted.

"Yes, I'm Thule," the old man said. "You can stay in my cabin. You will be responsible for the outhouse and the pig sty and for the cleaning and keeping everything in order."

"Whatever you want," Hume said. "But if I discover that you're not Thule, all hell will have to be paid."

Hume discovered in his work the perfect foil for his undisciplined thoughts. The more he resented the menial nature of his tasks, the more he asked himself whether he was worthy, at this time, of a higher position. He quickly recognized how his noisy mind interfered with learning. He never knew how much anger was in him until he had to clean out the pig trough. Every time he cursed the pigs or thought of running away, he tried to find something positive in the situation. But his unruly mind was like an animal kicking and biting at everyone and everything.

"The mind sees only half the truth at any time," Thule said. "Never trust it."

One hot August day, late in the afternoon, while working in the sty, Hume saw a lame man limping towards him from across the field. The man stopped for a moment and watched Hume work. Then he called out, "How far is the village?"

"Take this road five miles south," Hume replied, "in that direction."

"Obliged," the man said and turned away. Hume stopped working. He watched the traveler hobble down the road.

"Five miles must be an endless journey to him," he thought. "And I'm complaining about a little pig shit. It's a miracle that I can work, that I have arms and legs, and the strength to help Thule.

He put the shovel down, got into Thule's car, picked up the lame man and drove him to the village. When he returned to the house, Thule was standing on the porch.

"Thank you, old man," he said to Thule in a very humble way, "for having patience with me, for giving me time to understand."

Then he chased the pigs and goats around the yard and began to sing a song he had learned from his mother. From that day on, he stopped judging Thule; he was able to accept the old man's teachings and absorb them; and he grew to love Thule for his wisdom and humanity.

"If you learn to see the world as a reflection of yourself," Thule said to him late one afternoon, "you will allow it to become your teacher.

Thule still gave Hume difficult and baffling tasks and Hume found himself accepting the tasks with less anger and frustration. He also found that Thule was spending more time with him discoursing on all manner of things that pertained to the inner nature of man. "The only real freedom in life," Thule said to Hume, "is freedom from oneself. Whatever you understand can become your limitation if you accept it as the ultimate truth. One learns by way of paradox, which defies the rational mind and teaches us that spiritual energy has a logic all its own. It was such a relief for me when I discovered that there was no ultimate truth. I no longer had to explain it to eager disciples or myself. There's only energy, Tobias, and we all live our lives at the center of creation. The only thing missing is consciousness. For some insane reason, we've left it in an outhouse and it's slowly rotting from disuse."

At one moment Thule spoke about the beauty and joy of life, and the next he would rail against human stupidity. If he told Hume that he loved and valued him, he would then qualify it by calling him a child and a fool and would threaten to throw him off the island.

"Positive and negative are just states of mind," Thule said.

It was a late August afternoon and Hume had just finished digging trenches in a half-a-dozen locations on the island. He had no idea why. But it didn't matter. The work enabled him to get closer to Thule and to receive from him an endless stream of wisdom.

"If you accept one as the truth," Thule continued to speak, "the other will come along moments later and bite you in the ass. It doesn't matter if you are right or wrong, only that you are growing as a human being. As long as you cling to one notion of the world, you're a dead man. You're trapped in a circle of familiar things, and can find no way out."

After years of inner struggle, Hume began to see great changes in his own nature. He loved Thule's contradictory stories, and saw wisdom in paradox and stupidity in judgment, and he learned to find something of value in any situation.

"The true nature of growth," Thule told him, "is in conflict. If you stop feeling inner turmoil, you're no longer confronting the obstacles to your spiritual enlightenment. The seeker after truth is a warrior, and his battlefield is strewn with pieces of his own ego and self-image. He'll continue to destroy them until the moment he dies. The one thing I can't do is to protect you from the world. You're here to learn what I have to teach, and live your life. I learned long ago that my teachings are worthless if you can't put them to use. The real test of whether or not you've learned anything from me over the last seven years will take place when you leave this island. Our work here is finished, Tobias, and you must prepare yourself to go."

"I've always wondered why you sent me away so many times before accepting me as a student," Hume said.

"When I saw you on the beach," Thule replied laughing, "I was elated. I'd finally been sent a real student, but I had to be sure it wasn't my own fantasy. So I sent you away."

"But five times?" Hume asked.

"Yes," Thule replied, "five times. I had to be sure. If a man is dying of starvation and smells food, he will find a way to get to it, but if that man devours the food on the spot, he would probably die of indigestion. Creative energy is so vast and of such an intense nature that it is impossible to consume it whole. One must nibble at first, and as one gets stronger, one can absorb greater quantities. We live in a world that values instant gratification. No one values patience and discipline, or understands that we must become masters of ourselves."

After Hume left the island, he taught in universities, prisons, hospitals, reform schools, and eventually he trained The Dancing Man.

Thule lived to be eighty-seven. He took no more students after Hume. He felt his work was finished. He enjoyed his old age and meditated in the silence he found so comforting on his remote island.

"It's strange, Joshua, to think of you as part of this lineage," The Elder said to me when he finished his story.

"How do you think I feel?" I said to him. "Years ago, you were Mr. Lewis — a great friend of my father — the owner of a delicatessen where I'd go to talk with you when things got difficult. Now you're The Elder and telling me stuff that could affect the rest of my life."

"The world changes, Joshua, thank God for that."

"I must see to Marthe," Rachel said. "It's getting late."

In the dim light, she looked more like a specter than an actual person. She hugged The Elder, walked towards the door, but before she left, Rachel asked me to come to her apartment.

"As soon as you're finished here," she said. "I need to speak with you about something."

On my way out of The Elder's chambers, I recognized the old man and his grandson Tom sitting on a bench near the door. I waved to them, but they were so intent on speaking with The Elder, they didn't notice me. I decided to find Rachel's apartment, but in the corridor, I heard a voice reciting these lines:

"High on a mountain where the air is thin, I met an old man who lived by himself."

It was my old friend Ramon whom I hadn't seen for several years. He was now a young man of middle height whose full lips, aquiline nose and black hair punctuated a youthful face. There were lines and wrinkles etched into an impish countenance out of which his mischievous eyes twinkled. He wore faded jeans and a navy blue tee shirt. We shook hands, hugged and talked about our childhood in the Bronx. I had often thought about him and wondered what direction his life had taken. Happy to see him again, our conversation became more animated and intimate, and it was like old times.

He loved the streets of New York. The monumental indifference of the place allowed him to be himself. No one cared if he dressed outlandishly, worshipped the primordial ooze, or wrote love poems to the Statue of Liberty. He had once costumed himself to resemble the Hindu god *Siva*, and sat near a fountain in Central Park. Within minutes, orange-haired men and women with spiked apache cuts surrounded him. One guy dressed in a gorilla costume sat next to Ramon, and four jugglers and three mimes joined their group. Another man, who wore a long caftan and a fez, threw down a prayer rug and prayed to Mecca.

"I tell you, Joshua, it was better than the circus. An old man played an esoteric tune on a jew's harp, and I chanted an ancient Hindu prayer that my parents had taught me when I was a child."

"What are you doing here?" I asked him.

"The Dancing Man has many secrets that I want to learn," he answered.

Neither the Dancing Man, nor The Elder, nor Osmond had ever invited him to live in the building. But that never hindered Ramon's adventurous spirit. He had found a cellar door through which he secretly came and left; he was certain that no one else knew about the entrance. In two years of coming and going, he'd never met anyone that used the cellar door; nor was it mentioned to him by the people who inhabited the building. Ramon came at night and left in the morning. The Elder smiled whenever they met. Although he knew that Ramon wasn't supposed to be there, he didn't say anything.

"Yesterday, I sat on the steps of the 42nd Street Library and meditated for half an hour," he said. "Do you know that people dropped flowers in front of me, and coins, and one guy left a Bible?" The sun had warmed him and he could feel blood rushing through his veins and arteries and enter the hearts of pedestrians moving past. Radiant sunlight bounced off the street and rainbow–colored pigeons ate bread from the sidewalk.

"Were you stoned?" I asked him.

"So stoned I could barely move," he laughed. "I've become a little mad since we last saw one another. But I really don't care."

He once read about a monk who spent twenty years in a cave, and who decided that it was time to return to the marketplace and teach. The monk came down from the mountain, entered the walls of the city where he went from stall to stall and examined the fruits and vegetables, the clothing and household goods, took in the sights and smells, and listened to the cries of the merchants. A beggar grabbed his sleeve and asked him for a coin.

The monk became furious. He beat the beggar until the crowd pulled him away. There was bewilderment in the beggar's face. He looked at the monk. "May God have mercy on you," he said. The crowd glared at the monk until he walked away.

"Twenty years of solitude and profound meditation," thought the monk, "and here I am fighting with a beggar. I'm still a child. I should have come here to learn about life in the city, not to teach spiritual nonsense I picked up in a cave."

The next day, the monk returned to the marketplace and apologized to the beggar, and he lived there for over twenty years, befriending merchants and lawyers, beggars and holy men, and finally realized that there was nothing to teach. He learned that God lived in the marketplace as well as a cave.

Ramon studied the tenements and back alleys from a window in the main hall. "I've heard rumors that The Dancing Man has found a replacement and he's going to die," he said. "It's hard to believe after all these years."

"Who told you?" I asked.

"No one, really. You pick up a drift here and there."

"I just saw him dance. There was nothing in his movement to indicate sickness."

"I don't know if it's true," he said. "But there's talk of a new disciple, one who will be able to learn the craft."

"This is just a dream," I said to Ramon. "If I awaken, not only will The Dancing Man vanish, but Osmond, Rachel, The Elder and you as well. But I can't wake up, and I seem to be sinking deeper into my unconscious."

"I have to go to work," said Ramon. "Would you like to join me?"

"What do you do?"

"Come. You'll see. It's fun."

We walked through a maze of corridors and passageways until we came to a stairwell that went down to the basement. We left the building by an old, rusty door with a neon emergency sign on its lintel.

"Do you know where the garden is?" I asked him.

"What garden?"

"Where The Dancing Man sits in the afternoon."

"No," he said, "I didn't know there was one."

The tenements rose high above us like ruins from an ancient city, and we walked through the back alleys, climbed over fences, and turned into dark passages that connected the buildings. There were cats everywhere and an occasional stray mongrel eating garbage.

Ramon earned a living as a street entertainer. He sang and juggled and told stories to the crowds that gathered about him. When he wasn't entertaining or hanging around The Dancing Man's place, he was at a friend's studio painting or sculpting. Nomadic life fascinated him. It was free of convention. He knew that it was romantic foolishness, but he enjoyed it anyway. He wanted to tickle the funny bone of the world, and to see joy on the faces of people around him."

"Where are we going?" I asked

"Just over there." He pointed to a doorway. "On the other side is 174th St."

The street was throbbing with life. Ramon stopped at a produce market to buy some cashews. Housewives clustered about the store and shopped for fruits and vegetables. One old lady squeezed tomato after tomato. The shopkeeper was screaming at her, but she paid him no mind. The neighborhood sounds were like a well-orchestrated symphony from which I could pick out every instrument. When Ramon began to argue with the shopkeeper over the price of cashews, my head spun, and the store faded in and out of my consciousness. He finally came out carrying a bag under his arm.

"Want some," he asked me.

I took a handful of nuts and put them one after the other into my mouth.

"If I had to choose between art and The Dancing Man," he said to me, "painting and sculpture would win out. After I've finished a painting, it's easy for me to see whether I've changed or not. There's always an element of me in a landscape or in the smile of a young girl, or in a scene of ravaged streets in the South Bronx."

He once tried to paint a world so innocent that the concept of evil couldn't be found. A frightening idea, if you asked him. When he approached the canvas, his mind went blank. He couldn't even pick up the brush. Corruption was so deeply rooted in his life that the idea of paradise was an absurdity. How would he live there?

Ramon stopped at a corner and took three yellow balls out of his pocket. He cried out, "Ladies and gentlemen! Children too! Come! Gather round!" Many people seemed to be annoyed at the intrusion, but others stopped and watched. He began to juggle the balls with astounding skill. The crowd grew. He talked, laughed, joked and danced like a professional. Then he passed a cup and collected some coins. We continued to walk until we came to a quiet street where a few children played among the parked cars. Ramon waved to a young boy to throw him a rubber ball.

"Remember the games we played?" he said. "It's not so long ago."

"Yes," I replied and caught the ball as he threw it to me. He ran down the street and motioned for me to throw the ball over his head, and he made a one-handed catch, turned, and threw the ball to a teenage boy about fifty feet away.

"Does life repeat itself?" I thought. "This has happened before."

The boy laughed as he caught the ball.

"What does that kid care about death and the unknown?" I thought. "But how do you know? You've never spoken to him. You know nothing about his joys and pains."

The boy threw the ball back to Ramon.

"The crowds are just an illusion," I thought. "Every human being must face his destiny alone."

Ramon waited for me to catch up. He pulled out the three yellow balls and juggled for a moment, and put them away when I reached him.

"Most art today renders the banal," he said laughing. Then he told me that artists are afraid to reach into themselves to tap their own pure and untouched energy. They settle for a limited and safe view of the world. But the true artist accepts only the purest expression of his inner self, and doesn't mind excavating hundreds of dark secrets buried there. He's not an interpreter of life, but a visionary who has found a path to the truth. If an artist masters his craft, and isn't afraid of his own inspiration, every line, every color reveals the essential nature of the universe.

We walked through a vacant lot where huge boulders towered over our heads, and entered a cavernous passageway between tenements. I looked up at a building. There was a twenty–foot portrait of a naked woman with bulbous thighs and breasts painted on its facade.

"Is that yours?" I asked.

"No, it was done by a friend of mine," Ramon said. "He's driven to paint on any empty wall in New York City. Listen, Joshua, tomorrow morning I'm going to Manhattan to entertain. I need to make some money for canvas and paint. Would you like to come?"

"I'd love to."

"There's a strange character that shows up at almost all my events dressed as a clown or a skeleton or in a top hat, tie and tails, and he stands in the shadows and watches me," he said.

Once Ramon saw him on the subway. He tried to talk to him, but the train pulled into a station and the stranger got out.

"He's an incredible pickpocket," Ramon went on, "who never fails to slip five or six billfolds from the coat pockets of onlookers. He'll watch me perform, wave and smile, and disappear at the end of my routine."

Everything went well for Ramon when the stranger was in the audience. Sometimes he'd make over a hundred dollars for one performance. Last week Ramon threw a rose at him, and the week before, a chrysanthemum. The stranger caught each one, smiled, stuck it behind his ear, and disappeared in the crowds that moved up and down the street.

"When we entertain tomorrow, please watch for him. He'll guarantee us success."

Ramon and I spent a lot of time together. He taught me to juggle, to mime and dance, and to provoke an audience to laughter. We entertained crowds throughout New York City — near Lincoln Center, Central Park, Columbus Ave, and Washington Square. Each time, Ramon would whisper: "Look for my friend," and I would scan the audience and never see him. Ramon would then exclaim: "There! He's looking at us. Today will be a success." At the end of our act, when I passed the hat through the crowd, it came back filled with money.

"He was a skeleton today," Ramon said. We were walking past the fountain in Washington Square Park. "I first saw him behind a tree. Then he worked his way through the audience to the front, and I sang my last song for him."

He was a mystery to Ramon who had tried a hundred times to capture him on canvas and had yet to get it right.

"I've never seen him," I said.

"Of course not," he replied. "You're too caught up with The Dancing Man."

In the evenings, we'd practice until I mastered mime and modern dance. Ramon was a patient teacher. He gave me room to explore myself and find my sense of balance.

"I sometimes wonder," he said, "what it would be like to replace The Dancing Man."

"Perhaps you will have a chance."

"No," he replied. "He has never invited me through the front door. He nods at me occasionally, and I think he may respect my courage in finding a way in. But I'm too involved with myself."

He couldn't let go of that part of Ramon that wanted to be a star — the part of him that needed power and adoration. The Dancing Man didn't have to prove anything. He danced for the joy of it and surrendered every movement to a spiritual flow. The difference between them was very fine, but the practiced eye could detect it.

It wasn't easy to master his dance and juggling routines, but I trained every day until I learned them. When it came time to deliver comic lines, I was always at a loss.

"Don't worry," said Ramon. "One day you just won't give a shit. You'll find humor in whatever you see."

He picked up the three yellow balls and juggled them. "You have to get training," he said. "The Dancing Man can't live forever. Only God knows how old he is. I wouldn't venture a guess. Anyway, he needs a disciple, and I'm just too crazy for the job."

"I'm a novice," I said to Ramon.

"That qualifies you, Joshua. You have room to learn. You're not bloated with your own greatness."

"I'm full of confusion," I said. "And you have a freedom I've never seen before."

"Can't you see who I am?" he said. "I'm a little crazy, Joshua. My need to perform is more like an obsession than an act of surrender."

It controlled him to the point where he had lost touch with his own humanity. He'd watch his conflicting values as if they were two armies on a battlefield, and strange as it may sound, no one and nothing ever won.

"I just exhaust myself with tension," he said. "My need to create falls far short of perfection."

It was bound by a whirlwind of activity that never lets him sit still or direct his life towards selfless ends. It was impressive on the surface but not much inside.

"There's no balance in my life, Joshua, and I've got no right to be near The Dancing Man. My dance performances are a desperate attempt to free myself from I don't know exactly what."

He juggled the three yellow balls, whistled a lively tune, closed his eyes, and never once missed a beat.

"So pay attention to me, Joshua, because I'm not to be taken for granted. Though I've suffered greatly, I still appreciate every moment of my existence. But I tell you to be careful when you deal with me. All my outpourings of wisdom and generosity extend no farther than my need to create — and I sacrifice all relationships to it."

"Even our friendship?"

"Yes," he said. "I love you, my brother, but everything in life ends. That's the crazy part of it. Everything ends."

He returned the balls to his pocket, sat down, and said to me, "You've learned how to perform on the streets. Maybe tomorrow you can work the crowd by yourself."

Late the next morning, we took the subway to Manhattan. At the corner of Sixth Avenue and 8th Street, Ramon began to entertain. A crowd gathered, and after he introduced me to the audience, I juggled the three yellow balls. He turned on a tape recorder and motioned for me to dance. A little lost and insecure, I danced by rote, and fell back on the craft Ramon had taught me. When I finished there was scattered applause and we collected a little money. Then we took the subway to Columbus Circle.

"I didn't see your friend," I said to Ramon.

"He'll appear when you're ready."

"There wasn't much money in the hat."

"You'll have to improve your act," he said as we came to Columbus Circle. We went into a coffee shop, ordered two cappuccinos, and sat down at a table.

"A few years ago," Ramon said, "I submerged myself in the subculture of the city, living with pimps and thieves and junkies."

He believed that the dark, primitive world of city life would give him a glimpse into the unknown. He had read about sacred prostitutes in India — young girls who flocked to temples and were used by monks to arouse spiritual energy — a *Tantric* cult that helped *Saivite* devotees get closer to God. He believed some well-seasoned prostitute with a rose behind her ear could teach him the art of love, but quickly learned that survival was the keynote of all subcultural activity. If subculture had a flag, it would be the dollar bill. Allegiances don't exist there. Forced to reconcile himself to a solitary existence among companions who didn't care if he were dead or alive, Ramon lived in awe of Hindu saints that revered prostitutes as incarnations of Mother Kali. It was so distant, exotic and wonderful. But street life did teach him to survive and he also learned that people suffer no matter what level of society they belong to.

It was early winter, about two years ago, hungry and looking for food, Ramon tried to pick the locks of cars on the street and some tenement apartment doors, but had no luck. On top of a hill between 173rd and 174th Streets, a crowd had gathered to watch The Dancing Man. When Ramon saw him move beneath the streetlight, he knew, for the first time, what he wanted. It appeared to Ramon that his dance had captured the essence of all creative expression — perhaps even of death itself; and he returned every day for a year until he found a way into the building. He wanted to get close to The Dancing Man; he wanted to learn the secret of his dance."

"Maybe you will succeed him."

"No, I don't think so," he laughed. "I'm not next in line."

Two years of observing him had taught Ramon that his path led in other directions.

"You're a much more likely candidate than me," he said to Joshua.

"But I don't know anything about it."

"What you know is not important. All you have to do is develop the craft. The rest is evolution."

"And you're teaching it to me."

"Yes. In part."

"I'm not sure if I should thank you."

"You don't have to thank me," replied Ramon, smiling. "You just have to learn to dance."

Although Ramon was a childhood friend, he now lived in a reality that was strange to me. His words were sophisticated, but he wore his inner turmoil on his sleeve. He seemed to live in a self-imposed fairy tale, and the more he moved within its boundaries, the more lost he became.

"Most of life is trivial," he said to me. "We eat, sleep, watch television, take out the garbage, and perform a continuous round of chores that are mundane and boring."

Daily existence dulled the creative edge. There were too many empty spaces; there was too much time between memorable moments. We needed some filler.

"Just imagine if everyone knew the date of his or her death," Ramon said. "Just imagine if they knew how much time they would have before they left this world. Each moment would become precious. Even trivial things would take on a golden sheen."

"But people know that their time is limited."

"It's not the same," he replied. "There's a blind spot. People live with the illusion that death will never touch them. They live in hope and busy themselves with nervous activity and are eventually robbed of all they hold dear."

"Couldn't we do this without planning the date of our death?" I asked.

"Yes," he replied. "But look around you, just look around! How many people do it? There's a part of every one of us that dwells on the past and the future."

To his understanding, the past was dead, and the future hadn't arrived yet, and we focused on both of them as if they were some mysterious cure for life's daily ills. If a person decided that on a particular day, at a particular time, he was going to kill himself, he would quickly recognize that his time was limited and every moment left to him was precious and had to be enjoyed.

"You know something, Joshua," he laughed. "The mad and the holy often tread the same ground."

"Of course, the opposite could also happen," I said with some hesitation. "If we knew the day of our death, we might live the rest of our lives in despair. 'Why work? Why do anything? Life is absurd. I've chosen the moment I'm to die.'"

"There's no answer, Joshua, and the more I think about it, the more confused I become. It always gets back to the individual. There are no universal principles when it comes to death and dying. Just look at your father. He's found peace in the last hours of his life. Some people never do."

We left the coffee shop and walked to 74th Street and Columbus Avenue. The streets were very crowded, and Ramon expected to entertain a responsive audience.

"Ladies and Gentlemen!" he cried out. A few of his regular fans gathered around. "In my bag are wonderful tricks." He spent the next forty–five minutes juggling and telling jokes, singing and dancing, and the crowd grew. When he finished, I made my way through the audience with a big clown's hat and collected money.

We walked down Columbus Avenue to Central Park South.

"I didn't see my friend," Ramon said. He was nervous. "Something must be wrong."

"The take was meager," I said. "About twelve dollars."

"It's hard to perform when he doesn't show up," Ramon said as we walked along Central Park South.

"He'll be there tomorrow."

"I don't think so." He pointed to the top of the building across the street and said to me in a loud and very crazed voice, "Look at the serpent crawling up the facade of the Plaza Hotel. Have you ever seen a reptile spitting fire into an open pit?"

"Let's go back," I said and took him by the arm. "I think you need some rest."

"No," he said. He pulled his arm away. "The Dancing Man is a fraud and there's nothing for me to hold onto there. I'm afraid, Joshua. My friend didn't appear today, and I'm afraid."

"Let's go home," I pleaded with him.

"What for? I'm finished with that place. It's not my home." He stood still and continued to look at the top of the Plaza Hotel. "Serpents, yes, serpents," he said to himself in a whisper. "You know something, Joshua," he continued in a matter-of-fact voice, "I have to fix a date of my death. If I can, the vision of my life will clarify itself."

"Or become more absurd."

"Perhaps," he said and looked at me appraisingly. "You're learning very fast, and you, too, will someday see serpents."

He turned and walked away.

"Wait!" I cried. "Ramon!" I tried to follow him, but his walk became a run, and he disappeared in the crowd. After having spent hours looking for him, I finally found Ramon on the corner of Eighth Avenue and 42nd Street entertaining a crowd of curious onlookers.

"My friend still hasn't appeared," he said. There was a crazed expression in his eyes. "I'm not dancing right or singing right. I'm not going back into that burned–out building, Joshua. I have to move on."

"What will you do?"

"Get a studio," he said. "Paint and find my own vision."

"Where?"

"Soho, maybe, or Williamsburg."

"And The Dancing Man?" I asked.

"You love him because his dance captures the essential beauty that is at the heart of all things," Ramon answered. "His movement is like the wind in the sky, and I think he must feel the earth rotating beneath him. I would also like to dance like a force of nature, to love unconditionally and be loved by so many people. But what's really upsetting to me is that he asks for nothing and needs nothing in return, and I could never do that. I want too much out of life. I'm always questioning, always looking for reasons to be, and rewards, Joshua, I've got to have them. Every time that I see The Dancing Man, a certain calm overcomes me. It seems to be located at a mysterious point where life meets death; it's why I keep sneaking back into his house."

"But always through the basement?"

"I'm a thief, Joshua. I've stolen from him and he knows it. We have an understanding; we love one another, or, at least, he loves me, and I try to live with that."

The first year that Ramon snuck into the building, he stole something every night. There were always objects and money lying around. He grew to love the cat and mouse game that he played with The Dancing Man and The Elder, and the longer they played it, the more he realized that the two of them had left things in different places for him to steal.

"At first I resented his audacity, until it dawned on me that it was his unique way of allowing me to get close to him. I had never known such nobility of soul and the very idea of it made me stop stealing from him."

Though Ramon talked of doing great things, he had never done anything of value with his life. He didn't know whether he was an artist, a monk or a thief and he wasn't big enough of a person to be all three. He'd change costumes the way a chameleon changed colors. It didn't matter whether or not he was aware of all this because compulsion was the only thing that guided his life. Thank God that he didn't need to commit the perfect murder. He might have been driven to master that as well. The Elder once told Ramon that his gifts were his limitation and if he didn't develop an inner life, they would destroy him.

He was happiest when he stole from The Dancing Man. But something really strange happened. When he stopped stealing the objects and money he found scattered about the building, The Dancing Man and The Elder no longer distributed them for the taking.

"I still laugh thinking about it," Ramon said. "But, it's not enough for me to know that when I perform, I can make the people of this city laugh and cry; it's not enough for me to think that this helps me get a little closer to The Dancing Man. Every time I see him perform, I'm reminded of how little I really know. He doesn't let me hide from myself."

He broke off and walked away.

"Ramon!" I shouted. "My brother!" He stopped and looked at me. "There's got to be joy in what we do."

"Like The Dancing Man?" he asked.

"Yes."

"But does it work, Joshua? Is it possible to have a selfless devotion to mankind? Do people really want to change? There's a hagiography of crucified saints that says they don't. Think of how often a child grows up to be the splitting image of his or her parents."

"I thought you loved what you do."

"I do," he answered. "Does that make it easier?"

He also loved The Dancing Man, yet there were times that he wanted to kill him.

"How does he maintain his serenity and perform every night?" Ramon asked. " How does he go on as if time doesn't exist, as if age and death were just a joke?"

The Elder once told him that true teachings create conflict. They force you to work against yourself. A great teacher doesn't turn students into grazing cattle. He makes them see the dual nature of their inner lives — the love and hate relationship they have with themselves that they so often project onto him.

"The Dancing Man is like an incinerator burning everyone's garbage," The Elder said to Ramon the last time they were together.

"Let's go home," I said.

"No. I'll meet you later. I can't go back there right now."

"But he loves you."

"That's the problem," he replied. "You go on. I've got some things to do."

Three weeks passed. I returned to Manhattan almost every day and looked for Ramon in Central Park, on Columbus Avenue, Washington Square — our usual hangouts.

The summer sun's noonday light reflected from the windows of office buildings and people walked with umbrellas to protect themselves from its rays. I'd been out since 8:00 AM looking for Ramon, and there was no sign of him. I had almost given up hope of finding my friend. I crossed Fifth Avenue at 42nd Street and saw a crowd gathered on the steps of the Public Library. The moment I approached this large convocation of people, I heard Ramon singing an old chantey and saw him juggling three yellow balls. After he finished his routine and passed the hat, I went up to him. He gave me a big hug and said, "My friend was in the audience dressed like a clown. Things are going better now."

"I've missed you. I thought you would come back."

"It's over for me, Joshua. I've given up The Dancing Man. I've rented studio space in Soho and spend my evenings there. I'll take you to see it if you want."

We took the R train to Prince Street. The subway car was hot and musty and crammed with people. Bold and illegible graffiti was scribbled on the station walls and inside the train.

"I'm not going back to see The Dancing Man," Ramon said when we walked out of the Prince Street station onto Broadway. "A child must be weaned. He must learn to walk on his own feet, and I believe that many avenues lead to the same place."

His studio was a third floor loft in an old warehouse building. The space was large and divided by pillars. There were five eight–foot windows that looked out onto the street and let in a great deal of light. Many paintings, large and small, were scattered about. There was a consistency of theme in them — a sun or a fire into which processions of birds, animals and people moved and disappeared. Many of the figures in the paintings looked mythological.

"I've been experimenting with hallucinogens," Ramon said, "and have what I call 'sessions' every morning. They've opened me to mind–boggling experiences that give entry into the occult and the mystical. I often find myself seated cross-legged in the Buddha's heart. From there I watch my kaleidoscopic thoughts change in front of me. I focus on color and form and study them until they become part of my unconscious. Sometimes I'm afraid I won't exit the trance — that I will just dissolve into some kind of ethereal being floating through inner space."

Ramon poured a couple of glasses of wine. He looked tired and his eyes were glazed. He was not at all the person I had known in the Bronx.

"Do you want to go home with me?" I asked him. "We'll see The Dancing Man."

"I'm through with him," he responded. "There's no room for me there. Everyone loves him, but, for me to get close to him, I have to sneak into his house through the basement. I want my own vision of God — I don't need any intermediaries. If I kill myself, it's okay, Joshua. At some point, we all have to die."

He invited me to monitor his 'sessions.' Quiet and meditative, he'd swallow a few pills, then look at paintings or objects or out the window, and absorb himself in his own hallucinations. Though he sat perfectly still, his eyes were like two pieces of burning charcoal and I could feel an intense energy emanating from a place deep inside him — an internal force that slowly consumed my dear friend. Before one 'session,' Ramon told me that it wasn't important for him to eat when he took drugs. He could extract nutrition from the atmosphere. When not in 'session,' he'd live on a little brown rice and some vegetable juice, and in a very short time, his face grew skeletal, and his large eyes bulged from their dark and drooping sockets.

"You're very fortunate, Joshua," he said to me before one of his 'sessions.'

"Why?"

"The Dancing Man will teach you his art."

"You can learn as well," I replied.

"Me?" he laughed. "There's no way. It's too late for that."

The next morning, I returned to his loft, went to the cabinet where he kept the pills and put two of them in my mouth. Ramon cried out:

"You fool! You stupid little fool! What are you doing? You can't substitute this for the path you are on. I'm going to die! I chase skeletons in the streets! I'm mad, Joshua, and have no right to the vision of The Dancing Man. But you my brother, oh God, you've got to lie down on the bed. Why did you do that? These drugs aren't for you."

Within moments, my rational understanding of the world vanished. The room dissolved into a thousand particles as if I could walk through the walls and tables, as if I were in a mysterious world outside the realm of time. Ramon's breath moved in slow, rhythmic patterns that were like primitive chants resounding from the heart of a jungle. The entire room was ablaze with light and color. Each of my thoughts became a universe that I could enter and explore without limitation. I discovered in the vast recesses of my unconscious, eons upon eons of energy looking for a pathway into the world. My breasts swelled and I caressed myself and loved the sweetness I experienced within me. Spiritually pregnant, a fetus grew inside my belly, and a white bird flew out of my heart, circled the room and transformed itself into an ark. At the ark's helm was The Dancing Man. He smiled at me and steered the vessel towards a mystical place that manifested at the center of the sun.

Ramon took my hand.

"You will be the next Dancing Man," he said.

He bent over and kissed me.

"I love you, Joshua," he said. Then he drew me to him and we lay together, our bodies intertwined in a deep and long embrace. It was wonderful to feel his arms around me and to feel the warmth of his body next to mine.

"We're two children," he whispered to me. "We've created the earth and the sky and lie together in our painted palace of miraculous visions."

When the effects of the drug began to wear off, I heard Ramon say to me that he was going to dance on the street with a skeleton.

"I'll dance with him too," I said with a laugh. Then I closed my eyes and fell asleep. When I awoke, Ramon was gone. He left me a short note that read:

The movement of The Dancing Man
is the movement of the universe.
I've gone, Joshua,
to dance with my friend
who lives on the streets. — Ramon

My head throbbed with the after–effects of the drug and the room still vibrated. The many hallucinations that I had experienced were like hazy afterthoughts in my mind. It was as if all form and structure had dissolved and I had floated through the material world as one floats through water. Every thought, memory and sensation was held in abeyance. Exhausted and wanting to sleep longer, I forced myself to get up, take a shower and dress. "I'm going to see The Elder," I scribbled on a sheet of paper, then left his loft and walked to the subway.

The Elder was pleased to see me when Osmond and I entered his chambers. He shook my hand and gave me a warm hug. He asked Osmond to bring some tea. The room was now furnished with a long oak refectory table and a bench. Two large gothic windows overlooked the gardens in which I had once seen The Dancing Man lounging with Rachel and some other people. Osmond returned with the tea and The Elder and I sat in silence.

"I've missed you and Ramon," The Elder finally said. "Osmond told me of the 'sessions' you have at Ramon's studio."

"I only tried it once."

He sipped the tea and seemed to be contemplating the leaves at the bottom of the cup.

"How is Ramon?" he asked in a concerned voice.

"I'm afraid he's going to kill himself."

"He's too devoted to his visions and forgets our common humanity."

"Why don't you tell him?" I asked.

"I've tried many times," The Elder said, "but he won't listen."

"He's chasing skeletons in the streets, for God's sake, and filling himself with drugs. Ramon's so physically and mentally wasted that he's become a shadow of his former self. I love him, Mr. Lewis. He's like a brother to me."

"I know," said The Elder quietly.

"Then what's this all about?" I said. "Who is The Dancing Man? Why doesn't he do something? Why is Ramon killing himself?"

He studied my face for a long time and then spoke: "This is a dream, Joshua. You've conjured up childhood memories and have created a complex world for yourself — a place to hide from your ordinary life."

"But why?"

"You're looking for something almost impossible to find."

"So this is not real?" I asked.

"It's real," he said, "but this reality is linked to your unconscious. It will take you a lifetime to uncover the secrets of this dream."

"And you?"

"I'm Mr. Lewis, remember? I run a deli. I'm a friend of your father's.

I'm here because of your fantastic ability to dream," he laughed. "I'd rather be back in my deli waiting on customers. Don't you see? A man must dream. It alleviates the pain of life. It allows him the freedom to enter the unconscious and to use materials that are not available in ordinary living. It doesn't matter if Ramon or Rachel or I are real. The important thing is that you learn from us. We are your own creation, and we are here to serve you."

"Would Ramon's death be my creation?"

"Yes."

"And my father's?"

"No, Joshua. That part is not a dream."

After my interview with The Elder, I quickly descended a flight of steps into the basement, and left the building via the secret passageway. I wanted to see Ramon again. On my way to his studio, my mind reviewed our previous conversations.

"I'm a thief, Joshua. I've stolen from The Dancing Man and now I'm stealing from the universe. Maybe I'm God's fool," he said. "Maybe I'm a strung-out junkie who lives from 'session' to 'session.' Does it in any way matter that I'm trying to retain the innocence of a childhood I feel slipping away?

"Do you remember, Joshua, when we were kids playing in the streets? There was a carefree feeling about the way we approached each day. At what age did it all disappear? I just don't know anymore. Cunning as you think I am, with all my audacity and shrewdness, none of it is even close to the master thief called death. I steal objects and money, but death steals the very joy that's in my heart and it preys on every human being's innocence."

Each of his so-called 'sessions' gave him another glimpse of divine spirit. At the same time, it drained his vital energy. But he didn't care. All he wanted to do was dance with death. That was it. If he could just spin around the universe with this master pickpocket and tell him that he wasn't afraid of dying. Death, more than any other creature, should know that Ramon had seen the ethereal form of himself. It rode on the wings of a bird, and from the top of a mountain, it entered the sun; he should know that Ramon had seen the universe manifest as thousands of galaxies giving birth to one another.

"It's all energy, Joshua, moving towards the infinite. In a universe of that magnitude, even death has little or no significance."

A crowd had gathered around the loft building where Ramon lived.

There were fire trucks and police cars on the street. I fought my way through the onlookers to the front door, opened it, and ran up the stairwell. Two firemen descended the stairs carrying a stretcher. On it was a body wrapped in sheets.

"Who is it?" I asked.

"The guy who lived in there," said one of the firemen. He pointed at Ramon's loft.

"My God!" I cried out and pulled the sheet back.

"Do you know him?"

"Yes."

Ramon's face and neck were charred and almost unrecognizable. I put the sheet back.

"You finally did it," I said to him. "You've gone home." My eyes filled with tears. "Do not forget to be a child, my precious friend. I pray to God that you have found what you are looking for."

The next five hours were spent walking from downtown Manhattan to the South Bronx. The thought of Ramon's charred body was etched graphically into my memory and no matter how hard I tried, I couldn't erase it. He killed himself, I thought, and I should have known. He had told me in so many words that this was coming. I didn't know if I should feel guilty or just say, "The hell with it. Let the world be." What can you do if someone is determined to kill himself? Nothing, for God's sake, nothing but respect their insane wishes, love them, and let them move on.

It was 7:00 PM when I reached the top of the Bryant Avenue hill. The Dancing Man was performing and a large crowd had gathered there. I didn't stop to watch him, but entered the tenement building and went directly to The Elder's chambers. He opened the door when I knocked and asked me to come in.

"Ramon burned to death," I said to him. "It must have been during one of his 'sessions.'" The Elder asked me to sit down. "I loved him," I said. "He was like my brother."

"Yes, I know."

"Why did he play with death?"

"The mystery of it," The Elder said, "the idea of nothingness."

"I'm also intrigued with the mystery of it, I said, "but I'm not going to kill myself." There were tears in my eyes. "And now my body and spirit feel as if they're in limbo."

The Elder put his arm around my shoulder. "Ramon resented time," he said, "and he knew that it would continue with or without him."

That simple piece of knowledge made Ramon feel that his life was meaningless. He always talked about self-determination. He believed that if he knew the date of his death, each moment of his life would be more precious.

"I tried to reason with him, but never could," The Elder went on. "I once told him that if a human being has inner strength and balance, and is in touch with spiritual energy, it doesn't matter whether or not he knows the date of his death. He will hold each moment sacred. He will have respect for himself and for every living creature."

"But most people don't live like that," I said.

"Yes," he replied. "Most people live in a world without purpose, or set goals for themselves that are limited in vision. They need to be awakened to their inner lives; they need to understand that suffering reminds us that we are alive, and it may, if we're lucky, teach us to have compassion for others."

"But suffering doesn't ever seem to end."

"Why should it?" he replied. "Because you want it to; because you don't like it? How foolish to think that life should conform to your point of view. Most tragedy is remote from us. We read about it in the newspapers or see it on TV. Once in a while someone we know, like Ramon, dies, and it reminds us of our own mortality. There's no logic in it, Joshua. Just love him and let him be." He rose slowly and walked towards the door. "I've got to return to work now," he said.

"Why do you work so hard?"

"The Dancing Man saved my life. It's the least I can do in return."

After he left the apartment, I walked over to the window, looked at the empty garden below, and said softly to myself, "Thank you for your time and wisdom, Ramon. You spent your restless life searching for answers, and now, by God, I hope you've found them."

Rachel had become The Dancing Man's confidante. She prepared his food, ran errands for him, and took care of his apartment. She never complained. It appeared like she had put herself in bondage and compulsively fulfilled his every wish, and never once asked him for compensation.

At first, I was jealous, and very put out, but she just smiled when I told her my feelings.

"My life has to be shared," she said to me. "If I don't love you, Marthe and The Dancing Man, and fulfill my responsibilities in these relationships, my capacity as a human being will diminish."

She had discovered that there was a place in her heart for Marthe, The Dancing Man, and myself — a sanctuary in which those she loved could nestle; and that made her very happy.

"The first thing I had to learn was to trust that life's not an enemy — that people do love me and I can love them. None of us is guilty, Joshua, we just need to learn to love."

Rachel took Marthe in her arms, and the two of them rolled together on the bed.

"She's like a flower. She doesn't need a reason to love. She doesn't have to explain why she wants to hold me or kiss me. And I would trust her with anything."

Then Rachel kissed Marthe on the neck, and Marthe giggled and poked her mother's nose. They played like that for a few minutes, laughing and bouncing across the bed, Marthe draped across Rachel's neck, and Rachel laughing like a five year–old.

"People think I'm crazy to help The Dancing Man the way I do," Rachel said to me. She and Marthe were lying quietly on the bed. "But I don't give a damn. It's a privilege to serve him. It allows me to get closer to him, and in some sense, to be part of his dance."

She once believed that her loneliness was unique, but learned later on that it was a universal condition.

"You know something, Joshua," she said, "there's a part of me that won't accept fear as a way of life. I'll never allow it to keep me from loving you. You will never be a creature of my imagination. You're someone quite separate from me, and I must get to know you and respect you for the person you are."

Marthe crawled on Rachel's lap. "Mommy, sing me a song. Then can we go see The Dancing Man?" Rachel smiled at her and began to sing:

A child was born
on a summer's day,
and she and her mother
flew away
to a world of make believe,
to a toy maker's shop
on a little street,

on the other side of the moon;
she and her mother flew away,
flew away, flew away...

"The other day, I found myself yelling at Marthe," Rachel said. "Suddenly, I realized that I had completely forgotten what she had done to me. I was tired and probably more upset at myself than her. A few simple words would have been enough. She kissed me, and said: 'I love you, Mommy. Don't yell. I'm sorry.' She stood there with her two big brown eyes fixed on me. I picked her up. 'I'm sorry, little angel. Mommy loves you.'"

She looked at Marthe who was now running about the room flapping her arms like a bird.

"She and her mother," Rachel sang quietly, *"flew away to a world of make believe..."*

Then Marthe ran full steam into my arms.

"It's a beginning," Rachel said. "I remember you and me in high school when we'd sit and watch The Dancing Man perform. Now you're his disciple, and you will be given all his secrets. He's the only person I've ever met who has unconditional love for people, animals and things. Even today, it's hard for me to comprehend such an all–encompassing love.

"I know that this is a dream, Joshua," Rachel continued in a soft voice, "and you're wondering if The Dancing Man is real. Does it matter? Most of life is a fairy tale, anyway. It's like your initial response to your father's illness. You had spent your life taking him for granted and never once said to him, 'I love you.' Now that he's dying, you've become conscious of this man who has always been in your life. Isn't it foolish to overlook those who are closest to us, to forget that they are alive? We'd rather court strangers than pay attention to the people we love."

Marthe sat cross–legged in the middle of the room and drew animals on a sheet of paper. She brought a finished piece to Rachel and me. It was a horse. Its body resembled an undernourished rabbit and its head a tree. Its five legs were tiny, and its tail coiled around the horse's body and into the far corners of the picture. The sun shone above the horse on the right, and on its left, a silver moon beamed down. She gave the picture to her mother and began to work on another. Rachel and I looked at it and laughed.

"It's a long trek from the bottom of the hill to the place where The Dancing Man performs," Rachel said. She put Marthe's drawing on the bed and took my hand. "Every person has a different reason to seek him out, but to master his dance, we must learn to truly love. It means getting free of oneself — the real culprit," she laughed, "and live your life at the center of creation, and that's not a small price to pay. There are people who know nothing of life but pain and suffering. Do you remember Toni Lehman?"

"How could I forget," I replied.

She had a daughter about Marthe's age and they lived in an apartment downstairs from Rachel's parents. Her husband worked in a mortuary. He washed bodies or something. He used to clip the fingernails off of corpses and bring them home to Toni as a present. He'd always stink from formaldehyde.

"I remember he went fishing with a few friends and caught hundreds of flounders," Rachel said, "scaled them, cut off the heads and threw the meat of the fish back into Long Island Sound."

He returned that evening with a sack full of fish heads. Toni asked him what she was supposed to do with them. He shrugged his shoulders and said, 'Make necklaces.' He was fired from the mortuary and, unable to find another job, he earned a living by burglarizing the apartments of little old ladies. He tried to implicate Toni in his schemes, but she refused. After a six-month career of stealing from the aged, he was arrested, and sentenced to ten years in prison.

Toni tried to raise her daughter, but couldn't make ends meet. She began to drink and abuse the child, who'd often go hungry for days on end. The screams that came from their apartment were unbearable. Toni would beat Lisa to stop her from crying. One morning, the screaming was so bad that Rachel went to see what was wrong. Toni answered the door.

"Can I help?" she asked her. Toni didn't respond. Her make-up was smeared and her hair disheveled. She wore a dirty bathrobe. At twenty-three, she looked forty. Lisa just stared into space, and Rachel walked past Toni into the apartment.

"Will Mommy hit Lisa?" asked the little girl in a distracted voice. "Am I a good girl? Lisa is a good girl. Please tell Mommy not to hit her."

"Why do you hit her?"

Toni sat down on a bentwood chair. "You'll have to leave now," she said. "A client is coming."

"Toni!"

Her eyes were glazed, and she seemed to look through Rachel.

"Please," she said. "I am very busy."

"If you need anything, I'm upstairs," Rachel replied.

There was a knock at the door and Toni whispered to Rachel: "Poor John's a-growin' old. He left us here to fend for ourselves."

She took Rachel's hand and said, "I'll remember, but now you must go."

A few days later, Rachel climbed the apartment house stairs and heard sobs from Toni's quarters. She knocked at the door. There was no answer. When Rachel tried the knob, the door opened, and she walked in. Toni sat naked on the floor and her head hung between her legs. The room was in complete shambles. The dining table was overturned, chairs were broken, the stuffing from the couch was strewn about, and broken glass was everywhere. A dead parakeet lay in front of Toni.

"I killed her," she said, numbly.

"What?" Rachel looked at the parakeet.

"I killed my daughter," Toni said.

"Lisa!" Rachel cried and turned to see the limp body of a naked child. Her throat had been slit and she was covered with blood. Rage welled up in Rachel, and she grabbed Toni and began to shake her.

"Why? Why?" she screamed sobbing. "What did she ever do to you?"

The police came and took Toni away. She was convicted of murder and sentenced to life in prison. A year later, almost to the date of her conviction, Rachel went to visit her in upstate New York.

"I keep thinking about Lisa," Toni said, "of the moment she died, and I'll tell you something, Rachel, I loathe myself. I can't even stand the sight of my shadow."

She lit a cigarette and took a drag.

"Why did you come here?' Toni asked. "You don't have to worry. The guards beat the shit out of me all the time. They know I'm a child killer and I'm getting exactly what I deserve." She took another deep puff from the cigarette. "It's hard without a man," she continued. "I take a lover every now and then, but..." She looked at Rachel and started to cry. "My baby! Did you see her?" She backed away and her eyes were wild. "God, I miss her. Is there any word?" She came closer, and Rachel looked into her mad eyes and tortured face. "If you see her," she whispered, "tell her that I love her. Tell her Mommy loves her."

The next morning, Rachel brought flowers to Lisa's grave. She stood there for a long time in deep meditation, and decided that there's no sense in who lives and who dies.

** **

A shaft of sunlight dappled Rachel's face. She was beautiful, and I loved her dark eyes, her full lips, and aquiline nose. Her words came without effort, and her voice was musical.

Rachel slipped off her clothes and curled up under the sheets. She put her arms around Marthe and the two of them slept. I walked over to the window and looked out at a garden that was empty except for a few sparrows darting back and forth near the building. The summer sun had baked the trees and plants and walkways.

The Dancing Man stepped out from a door at the far end of the garden. He stopped walking and gazed thoughtfully at koi carp that swam lazily in a pond. Then he returned to the burned–out building.

"Joshua." Rachel called me. "Come here."

Her eyes were soft and loving and a white sheet was draped about her naked torso. Both of her arms reached out to me. I undressed and lay down next to her, and she placed one leg between mine and I could feel her nipples hardening against my chest. I kissed her parted lips. When she opened her mouth, her tongue touched mine and a warm sensation flooded my body. She made soft, sensuous sounds as I ran my fingers over her stomach and thighs, kissed her breast and circled her nipple slowly with my tongue. After we made love for a very long time, Rachel and I lay in one another's arms, and both of us fell into a deep, dreamless sleep.

The following afternoon, I met Rachel and Marthe in Central Park. Marthe was anxious to introduce me to a family of elves that lived on the Sheep Meadow. When we arrived there, she pointed to a large boulder.

"Over there," she said with breathless excitement. "That's where they live. There's one little guy named Crotchety, and he's going to take Mommy and me to the place where his parents were born."

"I don't think Joshua believes us," Rachel said laughing. She poked me in the ribs. "He's silly, Marthe. He's got no imagination." She took my hand in hers, and we scooped up Marthe, and the three of us wrestled a bit, fell to the grass, and rolled together to where the elves lived.

"I believe you, I believe you," I said, laughing. "Next time we'll bring some food and picnic with Crotchety. Do you think he'll let me come along to his parent's house?" I asked Marthe.

"I don't know," she replied. "Only if you behave yourself."

We lay on the grass together, tired, sweaty and happy.

"I love you," I said to Rachel and drew her close to me. Marthe crawled next to us and nestled against her mother. "I love her too," she said, "and I love you Joshua, and we can be a family."

"A beautiful family," I said, "and we'll always be together."

Marthe didn't reply, but she had a smile on her face that showed me how pleased she was with us being family.

"Look at the park's skyline," I said to them. "It's like a film set, and all the people lazing away the afternoon on The Sheep Meadow are extras in a movie starring the three of us. We're the center of the universe and our happiness makes us special."

"Will you take me to see that movie?" Marthe asked.

"Yes," I smiled, "both you and your mother."

At 7:00 that evening, I went to see The Dancing Man perform. There were loud cheers and handclapping when he walked onto the stage. He was dressed in black and wore a white mask, and after he bowed, the music began and waves of white light blanketed the stage. I could hear the chants of holy men fill the streets as if we were in a temple. The people on fire escapes resembled cherubs floating in space and The Dancing Man was transparent, untouchable, a wisp of a man more dreamlike than real. He bent over and planted a seed that became a tree, and its trunk rose higher than the tenement buildings and entered the dark sky. On each branch of the tree, I saw a different scene from my own life, and I knew, from a place deep in my heart, that I loved him, and that I would like to dance and share this love with all the people on the street.

Loud handclapping and cheers brought me out of my reverie. The Dancing Man stood center stage. He took a bow and raised his hands above his head. Many people in the audience shouted "More," but he was tired, and after his final bow, he blew a kiss and left the stage.

I followed The Dancing Man into the burned out building, met The Elder in the main hall, and he asked me to go with him to his chambers.

"The Dancing Man is ill," he said.

"I just saw him perform," I replied.

"He's been sick for months, but he refuses to cancel his nightly performances. Rachel's been taking care of him."

"Yes, I know. But she never told me that he was ill."

"I asked her not to," he said. "You weren't ready."

"And now I am?"

"Perhaps. What did you see out there?"

"It was strange, Mr. Lewis. A tree rose into the sky and on every branch there was a scene from my life; and you know something that was really strange — I had a deep urge to dance."

"A good beginning," he said smiling. "You still have much to learn, but thank God there's time for that."

⁂

It had been weeks since The Dancing Man made his last appearance on the street. The crowds had slowly vanished — disgruntled and complaining that they couldn't fill the void left by the discontinuance of his 7:00 PM performances. Word on the street spread quickly. The Dancing Man was ill, but no one could tell the exact nature of his illness or how severe.

"The Dancing Man wants to see you," Osmond said to me early one morning. I had just awakened from a deep sleep. "You must come to his chambers."

He led me through the building's corridors past The Elder's apartment and the clerical workrooms. Many people were gathered in the hallway — all of them in deep conversation about The Dancing Man. Osmond greeted each person as we passed. He was in excellent spirits and walked briskly beside me.

We left the burned–out building and moved along the garden path to a large house built in the shape of an ark. Red and blue dragons graced the bow and the stern, and a flag flew from each of its three masts — the foremost displaying a sun above a lake, and the rearmost, a moon and a flaming jewel. The central flag had a red ground. On it was a dancing female figure painted in gold. Her left foot stood on a dwarf and her right leg was lifted and bent slightly at the knee. She held a cup full of liquid in her left hand, and high above her head, in her right hand, there was a chopper–like instrument that pointed downwards. Though her face seemed fierce and uninviting, on closer inspection, her eyes had a soft and welcoming look. Osmond told me that Ramon had painted the three flags for The Dancing Man a few months before he died.

A pair of red, white and gold–painted bronze snow lions stood on either side of the entrance to the house. On the door itself there was a large painting of a lightening bolt. Osmond opened it and we went in.

The main room was furnished with hardwood benches along the walls and small rugs on the floor. Two six-foot gothic windows let in sunlight. An oak trestle table at the center of the room was crafted with large planks of wood, and a silver candlestick stood on either end.

"He's in the study," Osmond said. He knocked at the door and we entered to find The Dancing Man seated alone at his desk. He was dressed in a tight-fitting black outfit with a white mask.

He motioned for us to sit down. Then he raised his right hand and removed the mask and revealed a skeletal face of a man well over a hundred years old. It was wrinkle-free, and had two large brown eyes that twinkled with joy and love.

"I'm glad you've come, Joshua," he said. "When I first saw you on the street, I told Oswald that I had found my son. It has always been my dream to pass on the mastery of the dance. But it's taken so many scores of years for the universe to decree that the right time has come. Finally a son shows up — a child to whom I can bequeath thousands of years of teachings. Your parents, Joshua, were the vehicles that made it possible for you to come into the world, but I am the vehicle by which you will leave it. I've been dancing for a long time. I'm tired, my son, and ill, and I'm getting ready to die.

"All change is fundamental to life," he went on. "A tree surrenders its leaves and flowers, and gives birth to new ones. The wind erodes mountains and rivers carve pathways through the earth. Nature has time and patience. She is a true master of the dance."

I sat cross-legged in rapt attention at the foot of his chair and he told me that the body of a human being is a temple whose altars link it to a divine flow of spiritual energy. The mastery of the dance enables us to become aware of our inner lives and it reveals our place in the universal design. There are seven stages on which he performs, and each is located in the body, and when he moves from stage to stage, he takes the disparate elements of himself and unifies them. It's like a string of beads. When they're loose, they scatter in all directions, but threaded, they create a circle — a perfect whole. This, in essence, is the secret of the dance. Each of the stages is connected to the others by a flow of spiritual energy, and the dance is performed on all seven stages at once. His balance must be perfect — his mind clear and his heart open.

At first, he was puzzled by how few people wanted to learn the dance. But, in time, he discovered that each person does the work he or she was put here to do.

"I realized, Joshua, that when my dance is performed correctly, it embraces the dancer, the audience, and even disinterested persons; and I laughed, Joshua, I laughed for joy, because to dance on seven stages is an all–inclusive act of love. Just watch me as I move about the room."

He stretched his body and his slight and fragile frame grew into a monumental specter dancing in a ring of fire — his body transformed itself into a serpent whose three heads rose above the flames. On each of the heads sat a different figure: The Dancing Man on the right and Tobias Hume on the left, and both of them flanked by an archaic divinity with a rosary of skulls about its neck. Adorned with jewels, this deity was both masculine and feminine, and it carried a sun in one hand and a moon in the other.

The body of the serpent disappeared in a river that flowed through The Dancing Man's heart and to the crown of his head, a river that separated into three tributaries. They came together at a point in space where a recumbent female figure lay on a bed of clouds. A stream of milk poured from each of her nipples, and from her womb, she birthed myriad organisms that floated through space. There were humans, animals, insects and birds, and each, in its turn, entered the river that flowed past the seven stages in The Dancing Man's body and dissolved into nothingness.

"A river of spiritual energy makes the dance possible," he said to Osmond and myself when he finished his performance. He was now sitting at his desk. "It guides us into realms of consciousness that transcend time and space. The river flows from the womb of the Divine Mother, and reveals to us the beauty of creation."

Many years ago, he chose this place to dance. He thought that his performances would be solitary meditations on his own struggle to be free. But it didn't happen the way he had originally planned. First the wide–eyed children came and stared. Then the elderly came, and finally the rest of the audience.

"And now, Joshua," he smiled, "you will dance for them."

"I cannot separate you from my own father," I said to him.

"Don't try," he replied. "I've heard that the crowds have vanished, and only one young boy comes now."

"Yes."

"What time is it?"

"Seven o'clock."

"I must go."

"Where?" I asked.

"Where else but to the street, and I want you to join me. There's nothing to be afraid of," he said gently. He picked up a staff, and leaned on it as he walked.

"When you've learned to move on each of the seven stages," he said, "you, Joshua, will become a master of the dance."

"But you're too weak for this," I said in a concerned voice.

"That's all right," he replied. "Tonight you'll help me."

We walked together through the corridors of the burned-out building and exited by way of the main door onto Bryant Avenue. A young boy sat by himself on a blanket with his teddy bear. He smiled when he saw The Dancing Man. He was the only member left of an audience that once numbered in the thousands. Osmond turned on a recorder and music played.

"Surrender the image you have of Joshua," The Dancing Man whispered to me, "and love the world. The beat of your heart is the rhythm of life and death moving through time..."

He handed Osmond his staff, bowed to the young boy and danced. There was no sign of illness in him. His movement was strong and he took my hand and drew me center stage.

"Dance, my son," he said in a soft voice. "Don't be afraid. I will teach you everything I've ever learned."

There were no thoughts, no emotions and no physical pain. We danced together and shared the joy and love a son could only feel for his spiritual father.

"This inner quiet," he whispered to me, "this kind of nothingness is the source of all movement. It is here that you will learn to master your self." He paused for a moment and said, "as well as the dance."

A stream of unconditional love poured from his heart into mine, and we continued to dance together until I saw him collapse on the sidewalk.

"Don't stop," he said. "Dance, my child. It is as it has to be."

A crowd had gathered on the street and I danced from inner stage to inner stage. My heart swelled, and the love I felt was also unconditional and pure. When the music ended, there was great applause, and people cried out for more. The little boy handed me his teddy bear.

"I knew you'd come back!" he said. "I just knew that you wouldn't forget me."

** **

When I awoke, the morning sun had come through a window and pierced the still air of the hospital room. I stood up and stretched the stiffness out of my limbs, and leaned over my father's bed. He lay there in total stillness. His eyes were wide open and he stared at the ceiling. There was a smile on his face and a profound sense of peace about him. I kissed his forehead, and his lips, and sat quietly with him for a few moments.

Then I rose and left the room, and told the nurse at the desk that my father had just died.

About the Author

Stuart Perrin, an American spiritual master of Kundalini Yoga who has been quietly teaching small groups of students around the world for over 40 years, and is a direct disciple of Swami Rudrananda, more commonly known as Rudi. Stuart studied six years with Rudi. In 1973, Rudi died in an airplane crash and Stuart was one of three survivors.

Stuart Perrin was born August 10, 1942 in the Bronx, New York. The first child and only son of Sylvia and Michael Perrin, he began his spiritual quest at the age of sixteen. Sitting at his father's deathbed, he was shocked and awakened to a simple reality. "Why," he asked himself, "is it the first time I've seen my father in such a profound state of inner peace? Why did he have to wait until the last moments of his life to be filled with so much love and serenity?"

Stuart realized he'd have to find someone to train him in deep meditation practice. His search for a spiritual teacher took him to Europe, Africa, Mexico and all over the United States. Stuart spent nine years looking for a master only to find him in his hometown, where he met Rudi, who trained Stuart in the fine art of deep inner work and Kundalini Yoga. "What did you see when we first met?" Stuart once asked Rudi. Rudi answered, "I saw my spiritual son lost in the universe. I pulled you in the door of my shop."

Stuart's training with Rudi was filled with profound and ancient teachings, streetwise yoga, humor, and more than a few sword strokes to the ego. "See that weed in the sidewalk crack? It's got more life in it than you," Rudi once said to him while they were walking on a Manhattan street when Stuart complained to Rudi about his living situation.

After four years of intense training Stuart became a teacher in Rudi's lineage. Besides the formal technique of deep inner work, a technique that uses the mind and breath to strengthen the chakra system and build a link between the spiritual practitioner and Higher Creative Energy in the Universe, Rudi taught Stuart the necessity of using spiritual work in everyday life. "We must live here and there at the same time," Rudi told him. "If we don't master day–to–day living, we never work out our karma. We are never free."

Stuart taught meditation at Rudi's New York City center for two years. Then Rudi asked him to teach at a newly-formed meditation center in Denton, Texas. While in Texas, Stuart started meditation programs for hungry and homeless people, for people in prison and ex-offenders, addicts and ex-addicts, the elderly, high school students, and other people in all walks of life. He also initiated devoted disciples into the mysteries of inner work, and he, in turn, created new teachers of meditation.

In February of 1973 Stuart and Rudi were in a plane crash in the Catskill Mountains that took Rudi's life. "I never feel he is gone," Stuart wrote of his guru. "When I wish to be with him, to learn from him, I just open my heart. He is there, sitting, smiling, sharing his teachings. The moment he died, I felt his soul pass into me."

Stuart moved back to New York City in 1980 and continued his work as a spiritual teacher. He continues to train many more people, and has meditation centers in the U.S., Israel, and Brazil.

For more info:

stuartperrin.com

Made in the USA
San Bernardino, CA
01 April 2016